CW01496787

Not Making Hay

Not Making Hay

THE LIFE AND DEADLINES
OF A 'DIARY' FARMER

FRANK
McNALLY

Gill Books

Gill Books
Hume Avenue
Park West
Dublin 12
www.gillbooks.ie

Gill Books is an imprint of M.H. Gill and Co.

978 18045 8319 7

Design origination by Sarah McCoy
Edited by Neil Burkey
Proofread by Jane Rogers
Printed and bound in the UK using 100% renewable electricity at CPI
Group (UK) Ltd
This book is typeset by Palimpsest Book Production Ltd, Falkirk,
Stirlingshire

The paper used in this book comes from the wood pulp of sustainably managed forests.

For permission to reproduce lines from 'Epic' by Patrick Kavanagh,
the author and publisher gratefully acknowledge © The Trustees of
the Estate of the late Katherine B. Kavanagh, through the Jonathan
Williams Literary Agency.

For permission to reproduce lines from 'Digging' by Seamus Heaney,
the author and publisher gratefully acknowledge © Faber & Faber Ltd.

*To the best of our knowledge, this book complies in full with the
requirements of the General Product Safety Regulation (GPSR). For
further information and help with any safety queries, please contact
us at productsafety@gill.ie.*

A CIP catalogue record for this book is available from the British
Library.

5 4 3 2 1

Contents

Preface

ABOUT THREE YEARS AGO, HAVING been 'An Irishman's [or Irishwoman's] Diary' for almost a century, the daily newspaper column of which I am chief writer underwent a small rebrand. Henceforward, but in the online version only, it would go by the non-binary title 'An Irish Diary'.

The change provoked some interesting reactions, including a couple of protest Letters to the Editor from traditionalists. In the print edition, as always, those appeared on the same page as the 'Diary', so that the letter writers were complaining about the loss of a title that, in fact, was still being used there.

But an indirect and surprising effect of the online rebrand is that it alerted me to one of the more common typos in the world of agri-journalism. This is the tendency, when writers mean 'dairy', to type 'diary' instead, a mistake that spell-checkers (and many human sub-editors, clearly) fail to notice. As a result, whenever I googled the term 'Irish Diary', as I did occasionally from then on, the results could sometimes be alarming.

After Liz Truss became British prime minister, for example, and it was reported that she might trigger Article 16 of the Northern Ireland protocol (a post-Brexit agreement allowing the UK to make unilateral decisions on cross-border trade), someone on Twitter warned that this would have serious implications for the 'Irish Diary industry'. Meanwhile, and more reassuringly, RTÉ's news website announced that 'almost half of Irish diary exports now go to destinations outside the UK and the EU'.

But in 2023, even the estimable Brussels Correspondent

Tony Connelly was tweeting that a new regulatory scheme being considered by the UK would 'put a question mark over the circulation of NI diary products in the Republic'. Bad news there, apparently, for my occasional stand-in contributors from Belfast and Derry.

The confusion was not confined to Ireland. On the contrary, news from abroad could be even more worrying. As I now also noticed, vegans in Britain and the US seemed to hate columns such as mine. Hence the typical headline: 'Why the diary industry is much more cruel than you think'.

Then there was an American health website claiming that, while 'diary products' are a good source of calcium, they are also, in many diets, the main contributor of 'saturated fats', and thereby linked to 'heart disease, type 2 diabetes, Alzheimer's'.

On top of all that, the diary sector was (and still is) blamed as a major cause of climate change. Scurrilously, primary producers in the chain are said to emit 'vast amounts of methane into the atmosphere', although some of us have never even been tested.

A happier side effect of noticing the typo everywhere is that I have since come to think of myself as a diary farmer. The jobs have more in common than you might think. Hours are broadly similar, for one thing, comprising the entire waking day if you're not careful.

I too have to milk daily, after a fashion: herding ideas – often underfed – every morning and squeezing them for all they're worth, or more. Then I release them back into the fields overnight, or sometimes out onto the 'long acre', in the hopes that they will fill the quota again tomorrow.

In one way, diary farmers have it worse than dairy farmers. Robot milking, for example, is not yet a workable option in our industry (although with AI, it may replace us too soon enough). And unlike dairy farmers, who can delegate it to their cows, we must do all the grazing ourselves.

Fodder shortages are also a regular occurrence for columnists, despite the mountains of books, magazines and newspaper cuttings with which we fill our working (and living) spaces. You can never have enough ideas to guard against writer's block. Which is why I agree up to a point with those dyslexic vegans. The diary industry can indeed be cruel, if only to diarists.

Readers (not to mention my late father, who was an actual dairy farmer) might think it rich to compare the privilege of writing a daily column with that job, or indeed with real work of any kind. Then again, the sainted Seamus Heaney did something very similar. Remembering his forefathers digging turf, he likened it to the scratching of his pen on paper and the excavation of ideas for poetry:

… But I've no spade to follow men like them.

Between my finger and my thumb
The squat pen rests.
I'll dig with it.

Not that I expect a Nobel Prize for such insights as the dairy/diary parallel. Still, just in case, let me also mention here another Nobel laureate who comes up a lot when you Google 'Irish Diary'. I refer to the German writer Heinrich Böll, who won the prize for literature in 1972. There is no typo involved in his case, because 'Irish Diary' is one translation of the title of a famous travelogue he wrote about his time in Ireland during the 1950s: *Irisches Tagebuch*. But given the extent of the dairy/diary confusion, I am both pleased and amused to find a Böll among the cows, as it were, and hope his presence will improve the milk yield eventually.

That, by the way, reminds me of another alarming example of the agri-journalism misprint I saw recently. Lamenting the waste of resources (and of bovine life) in industrialised milk production, someone asked: 'How about Irish Diary becomes a world leader in sexed sperm to minimise male calves ...?'

Addressing such confusions for my *Irish Times* readers a while ago, on behalf of the 'National Diary Council', I attempted to reassure them that:

> ... except for a few columns involving overseas flights, Irish diary products are not to blame for melting the ice caps. Nor do diary products cause heart disease, diabetes, or any other known health condition.
>
> Some users may experience mild irritation from time to time, it's true. But taken in moderation, preferably with breakfast, a daily diary can help prolong your life, or at worst make it feel that way.

Joking aside, readers of this memoir may notice two broad themes united by a common misprint: a rural upbringing that marked the author for life, and an adulthood in Dublin, the last 20 years of it writing daily dispatches for a newspaper.

It was the sound of a spade under his window in rural Derry that inspired Heaney's favourite poem. By contrast, the sounds from under my city window these days are traffic, tour guides, the bells of Christ Church and rapacious Dublin seagulls.

That incidental everyday life of the city does provide plenty of material for a daily column. But I'm also often drawn back to the Ulster drumlin dairy farms of my childhood. And like the great poet, in my own way, I do a lot of digging.

Home

OURS WAS A SUBURBAN FARM, located just on the northern edge of Carrickmacross, on the road to Ballybay. From the late 1960s onwards, the town was stretching out past us in a string of bungalows. We soon had a footpath at our front gate, and streetlamps to light it at night.

From the tile factory just down the road, opened by a French company in 1969 on what had been one of our fields, we also had the low hum of industry permanently in our ears. But we were farmers even so, and therefore country people. We would never go to the Gaeltacht on summer holidays from school, for example, or on summer holidays generally. Those were for townies.

Although only 45 Irish acres – or 60 'statute' as they used to say – it was a farm of two halves, separated by the ridge of a classic Monaghan drumlin. From the top of the steep hill behind us, there was a spectacular view down across the bungalows and eastwards over Monaghan's basket-of-eggs landscape towards Slieve Gullion in South Armagh, and beyond that to Dundalk Bay and the Cooley and Mourne mountains.

The other side of the hill had a lonelier view, westwards towards Cavan. There were drumlins there too, of course, broken into little square or triangular or rectangular shades of green, like an Impressionist painting. But there were no mountains, and few houses of any kind.

Our fields back there all had their own names, the most romantic of which was 'Cornfield', although I never saw any corn in it. That was the highest part of the holding, a rectangular plateau on the drumlin ridge.

Others were identified by proximity to neighbours: 'Lennon's', 'Cassidy's', 'Kerley's'. One was christened 'Poll Mór' by my father because there was a big hollow in the middle of it. The hollow got flooded in winter. I remember a duck swimming in it once as we gathered potatoes on the lake shore.

A small bog marked the boundary at one end of the farm. It had a wild gooseberry bush and a couple of blackcurrant ones on our side that we harvested annually for jam, if the neighbours didn't get to them first.

Across the bog was a field with a big rock sticking up in the middle, where an elderly neighbour was often seen to kneel and pray in the evenings. The story was that he had seen an apparition there once. I presume it was the Virgin Mary, but I never had the chance to ask him.

That part of the farm we had bought after the previous owner died, just before I was born, his immediate family having all predeceased him. His house was half a mile from the road at the end of a long, winding lane. It must have been a lonely place sometimes, especially for a man who had lost his wife and children.

Now the lane was overgrown, and the house and its walled garden deserted. Plum and damson trees still sprouted fruit every autumn. But it was a lonesome and eerie spectacle in the evenings whenever I had to go there to bring the cows home.

It can't have been more than a 15-minute walk from our house to the farthest corner of the farm. But partly because of the steep hill in between, it felt like another world out there.

When you were working in the back fields, especially in hay-making season, it could be for the whole day. We wouldn't usually start until after dinner – which of course was at midday – anyway. But once there, it was unthinkable to return to the house for meals. Instead, my mother and some of my five sisters would bring tea and sandwiches out to us.

There was an old covered well in a neighbour's field from which, on hot summer afternoons, we would sometimes get drinking water. One day I went there to fetch some and a rat jumped out just ahead of me. That was the last time I ever drank from the well.

I remember long, sweltering days when the arrival of 'the women with the tea' was awaited like a humanitarian rescue mission. We would gaze at the horizon anxiously as hunger and thirst worsened. Even my father would ask: 'Any sign of them?' Then, finally, the female cavalry would come slowly over the top of hill, to relieve the garrison.

Turf cutters claim that tea never tastes better than on the bog. I can't comment on that from experience. But tea in a hayfield at the height of summer is hard to beat too.

Now and again on hay days, we would be out in the back fields until nightfall, or nearly. Those days had an epic quality, and the journey home might as well have been from a foreign country.

A scrap of memory lingers of one such occasion from early childhood. It's a fleeting moment on a July or August evening, divorced now from whatever happened before. I'm sitting on the mudguard of my father's Fordson Dexta as we chug along across the brow of Cornfield.

I can still smell the tractor. If I try hard enough, I can smell my father's coat. We are returning like heroes from some Herculean day's work. The darkness is closing in on the lonely fields behind us. But just ahead is the top of the hill, and beyond that the welcoming lights of home.

***

It was the end of the self-sufficiency era, before specialisation became the norm, when farms still produced a bit of everything. We usually had a field of potatoes, and one of barley or wheat.

A clutch of hens supplied all the eggs we needed. We drank our own milk, unpasteurised of course, sometimes still warm from the cows so that it formed a froth on your tea. We even had an apple orchard, somewhat overgrown.

For a time, we also used to keep a single sow, which produced an annual litter of what were known elsewhere as piglets or bonhams, but that we called 'gurries' (a word I have never heard anywhere other than Monaghan).

That was until a blackly comic event, sometime in the late 1960s, when we were letting the sow into the field across the road one day, and she was hit by a passing Denny van. At least I think it was a Denny van. My older sisters insist it was from Castlebar Bacon. Either way, it was a dark joke.

Happily, the sow wasn't killed. On the contrary, being pregnant at the time, she went on to produce another healthy litter.

In the Ireland of that era, nobody sued for damages. Instead, whenever he passed our house for months afterwards, the van driver dropped in with a present of bacon and sausages. I presume the poor sow ended up as rashers eventually. She was never replaced.

In my earliest years, we still milked cows by hand. I managed this trick once or twice, with difficulty: you had to simultaneously squeeze and pull, but smoothly and with rhythm. If the cow didn't like your technique, she wouldn't cooperate.

My mother was an expert, of course, like the six-year-old Patrick Kavanagh's mother. I too have heard the 'music of milking', as mentioned in his poem 'A Christmas Childhood'. But then we got a milking machine to do the job, Swedish-made by a company named Alfa Laval.

That was musical too in its own way, albeit the music was confined to one note. The motor made a sound like a vacuum cleaner, but lower and softer. As heard across the yard outside the byre at evening time, it had a deeply soothing effect. It meant the cows were in for another night, there would be milk tomorrow, and all was well with the world.

Farming wasn't all idyllic. There was also a lot of casual cruelty involved in it then, none of it deliberate, it must be said. Male baby pigs had to be castrated by the vet, for example. I recall some kind crude anaesthetic being held to their noses, but they still squealed horribly. I can empathise with Clarice Starling in the film, except in my case it's the silence of the hams I'd be wanting.

Bullocks not intended for a breeding career – which was all of them by then, the AI man (artificial insemination, not intelligence) having taken over the task of impregnation – had to be castrated too. And that was a rather crude business.

I hope the vet gave them something in advance. Either way, I'll never forget the sight of a pile of bovine testicles outside the shed where the operation took place. They replaced the procedure with something called 'squeezing' soon afterwards, which seemed marginally more humane.

But we loved our animals too. The cows were still few

enough back then that we gave them all names. The calves were dotey little things. If a new-born one was sick and the weather cold (which it usually was, calving season being in January/February), we would sometimes bring it into the house for a day or two.

The patient would be installed in his own little manger in a corner beside the kitchen range, with an infrared lamp for added warmth. It would probably be suffering from scour, the details of which I'll spare urban readers. But we didn't care. It was a like a living Christmas crib, without the Holy Family. Or maybe *we* were the Holy Family.

The loveliest thing of all, though, was the chicken house whenever there was a new brood just hatched. They would have an infrared lamp too. But they also had to be protected from draughts.

So there was usually a heavy curtain, improvised from old corn sacks, across the front of the coop. That transformed it into a magical grotto. Pulling the curtain back, as children, to peer in at the little yellow bundles of new life under the lamplight inside was a spectacle no theatre could ever match.

***

Christmas apart – and it ran that close too – the best day of the year in my farming childhood was thrashing day, when our field of oats or wheat or barley was put through the mill.

This was before the coming of combine harvesters, or at least before anyone in South Monaghan could afford to buy one. The mill in question was one of those old wooden-framed contraptions that were run off the belt-drive of a tractor: now extinct except for occasional appearances at heritage events.

Like Christmas, thrashing day had an eve of anticipation – the night before when, usually, the touring mill would arrive from its previous job. Parked overnight in the haggard, its strange, hulking silhouette looked a bit like a dinosaur, which in a way it was.

That was the start of the excitement. Then the great day would dawn, and most of the neighbourhood would be involved. Unlike combine harvesting, thrashing was a communal event, like an Amish barn-raising. Most of the men in the locality would lend a day to it, even though there wasn't work enough for half of them.

That wasn't the point. To paraphrase Milton, they also served who only stood around talking and smoking cigarettes (barley and wheat seemed to be less flammable then than today). As our local poet Patrick Kavanagh had put it in his poem about the phenomenon, decades earlier, they were 'paying bills of laughter / And chaffy gossip in kind'.

Of course, working or not, they all had to be fed. And for the likes of my mother, the logistics of this, and the stress levels, probably did surpass Christmas. My older sisters were a great support, I'm sure. But not all her children were so helpful.

I remember one infamous year she ran out of butter, mid-dinner, and had to put out Stork margarine in its place. For a self-respecting housewife then, this was an occasion of deep shame. Cholesterol hadn't been discovered yet (round where we lived anyway), and margarine was still only for cooking. No normal person ate it, voluntarily. But needs must, and my mother hoped the guests wouldn't notice, or if they did, that nobody would pass comment.

And nobody would have. Except that, distracted by her catering crisis, my mother had committed the unforgivable act of refusing me the place among the men that my station demanded (I was seven or eight at the time).

So, hell having no fury like a small boy scorned, I sneaked up to the table with the Stork-infected butter dish, and blurted the truth, before my mortified mother could choke me. As I discovered that day, hell had at least one greater fury than a small boy in a huff.

Still, I prefer to dwell on non-violent memories of the era: the laughter, the conversation and the profound if fleeting happiness that came with saving the harvest.

I have to disagree with Kavanagh, by the way, when he suggests that 'carrying bags' was 'the best job at the mill'. On the contrary, having been briefly promoted to it a few years later, I would argue that there was no mill job to compete with being up on the platform, feeding sheafs of corn down into the jaws of the machine.

There, not only did you lord it over those on the ground, you also basked in the glory of perceived danger. A wrong move and you might feed your leg in instead. However slight the risk, it added to the glamour.

Normal rules were suspended on threshing day. I recall, for example, within minutes of my elevation to the mill-top, being embarrassed to lose my father's second-best penknife into the machine. But even that, it turned out, was an occasion for smiles.

You weren't a proper mill-man until you'd lost at least one penknife, I was assured. The main thing was to hold on to your legs. In the meantime, it was a good idea to tie the next knife to your wrist, as veterans did.

As for carrying bags – big jute bags, filled with grain – I never had that privilege. They were bigger and heavier than I was for most of my milling career. By the time we would have been a match, the old-style threshing had gone the way of all dinosaurs.

***

As in most country houses of the time, ours had a room known only as 'the Room'. Townies might have called it the 'sitting room' – and we did sit in it sometimes – or the 'living room'. But we didn't do much of our living there, as a rule.

The Room was where we kept the family pictures, mainly. It tended to be cold unless there was a fire lit, which was seldom. Only when you were oppressed by the anarchy of a seven-sibling household might you seek asylum there.

When well pre-heated, with a fire in the grate, the Room was where we received any VIP guests. Its finest hour was an occasion circa 1969 when my father – a Fianna Fáil councillor – allowed us stay up past bedtime one night to meet a man who arrived in a chauffeur-driven car.

The guest had a posh, anglified accent, so much so that for years afterwards, my mother delighted in doing a bad but affectionate impression of the way he pronounced the word 'butter'. His name was posh too: Erskine Hamilton Childers.

But he was our TD then, parachuted into Monaghan as part of a plan to persuade the local Protestants to vote Fianna Fáil, for a change. When they didn't have an independent Protestant candidate to support, Fine Gael tended to be their default, as the lesser of the main two evils.

Not only was he a government minister, Childers was soon to become President, earning my parents a ticket to the inauguration ball in Dublin, an event whose grandeur put the butter-pronunciation incident in the shade.

In the meantime, that night we got to shake the hand of a man (as I only learned years later) who shook the hands of the men in the Free State government who ordered his father's execution in 1922. When they met for the last time, Erskine Sr had asked his teenage son to do this whenever the opportunity arose.

The kitchen, meanwhile, was where we lived. It got very crowded sometimes with seven children. But it was cosy. In the years before we had central heating, the range exercised a magnetic attraction, especially in winter.

The kitchen was also where my father held court as a county councillor. He occupied the power seat – in the corner farthest from the door – beside a press in which he kept pension and planning application forms, stuffed into an old, cube-shaped biscuit box from which the pictures had long disappeared.

There were no official visiting hours. People called morning, noon and night. No time was sacrosanct. I remember occasions when we'd be driving out the gate to 12.30pm Sunday mass, cutting it fine, and somebody would drop by with a favour to ask.

As my father rolled his window down, my mother would be rolling her eyes in the opposite direction. Sometimes it would be a short, easily dealt-with query. Other times, it might merit my father lighting his pipe to think about it. Then we were in trouble.

The concept of privacy had not caught on in Ireland yet, at least not where we lived. People called unannounced. And unless they were salesmen or other strangers, they called to the back door, not the front.

Our kitchen was often the scene of the ancient Irish

tea ceremony (which, like the Japanese one, should be refined as a cultural treasure and performed in formal settings for tourists). This began, typically, with the visit of a neighbour who would stop just inside the door and say, 'No, I'm not coming in', when offered a chair.

A few minutes later, the visitor might advance as far as the kitchen range, still refusing a seat. Finally, they would relent and sit down, but often only after moving the chair nearer the door, to show that the original plan had not yet been abandoned. At this point, my mother would offer tea and something to eat. The response to which, always, was: 'No, I'm only up from the table.' And so it began again. The ceremony might conclude with the guest having dinner. But this would never start within 15 minutes of arrival, and reluctance would be protested till the end.

Our house, which had been built by the grandfather I never met, was perpendicular to the road, on an east–west axis. Accidentally or otherwise, this was in keeping with a common practice in Ireland which once, at least in western parts, had supernatural significance.

In Gaeltacht areas, 'the Room' was also known as 'the west room', invariably being situated at that end. That was also the direction to which local 'fairy paths' were ascribed. Food or water was sometimes left there at night.

A Harvard scholar who studied the subject in 1930s Clare noted that no outhouse or shed was ever added onto that gable. Such a building would be 'in the way', he learned. Of what was never specified. But among the 26 houses in the area he lived in, none had a shed on the western side.

Wakes were also usually held in the west room, suggesting a link with the setting sun. Bad luck was associated with extensions to that side. In parts of Mayo, they were said to bring 'death within a year'.

The modern bungalows that surrounded us by the 1970s were almost all, by contrast, parallel with the road. But deliberate or not, our east–west plan was where fidelity to tradition began and ended. 'The Room' was on the eastern side of the house. And bad luck be damned, we had sheds at both ends.

***

The other landscape of my childhood was 'Auntie Mary country', named for my mother's oldest sibling and only sister. It was barely three or four miles away from home. But it was across the county border, in East Cavan, and approached along increasingly narrow, winding roads.

It was at high altitude too: half-mountainy, with poor land on which only rushes seemed to thrive. Even though we could see our native Carrickmacross from up there, it seemed very far away.

When we were farmed out to Auntie Mary and Uncle Jamesie for Christmas and summer holidays, it was like going into exile. We used to write letters home and give them to the postman, waiting for him as he passed the end of the lane in case he had nothing to deliver.

They even had a different language up there. Or at least the Ulster Scots that had died out in Carrickmacross was still widely used. A hill was a 'brae' in those parts. A drain was a 'sheugh'. A door was a door, even there, but it rhymed with 'sewer' not 'sore'.

Auntie Mary was a bit of a puritan. A woman of spartan work ethic and strong opinions, she dispensed many and often disapproving judgements on issues, such as skirt length, hairstyle or behaviour, that fell under the remit of 'losing the run of yourself'.

But being childless herself, she was also the classic indulgent aunt. At home, it was always a seven-way fight for a thin slice of every cake or apple tart. Auntie Mary thought nothing of you eating half or a whole tart, and baked accordingly.

In turn we used to carry water from the well – located among the rushes in an adjoining field – for her every day, until the group water scheme connected her to the mains in the 1970s. Even then, water was not something to be wasted. We were warned not to flush toilets unless strictly necessary. Using the indoor toilets at all was optional.

We helped in other ways we could too. One day, me and my younger brother Padraig insisted on taking the creamery cans down to the road to be collected, via an upright wheelbarrow. The plan worked well as far as the bend in the lane, from where the trajectory descended steeply to the road.

There, alas, the heavily laden wheelbarrow ran away with us. An aluminium can pitched forward, losing its lid and unleashing a river of milk down the lane before we could retrieve it.

Fearing the wrath of Auntie Mary, which could be biblical on occasion, we immediately launched a cover-up. That was easier said than done. But we used our jumpers to mop up as much of the evidence as possible.

Then we considered adding water to what was left of the milk (something farmers were known to do on occasion, although it had to be after the roadside quality test, carried out by the tanker driver, which was the tricky part).

In the end, we gambled that the shortfall would not be noticed until the next cheque from the Co-op, by which time we'd be safely back in Monaghan. I think we got away with it.

***

Auntie Mary's husband, Uncle Jamesie, was off working most days. He drove a lorry for 'the Gyp': Gypsum Industries, near Kingscourt. Used to make plaster and dry wall, the mineral was mined in nearby Magheracloone, our maternal homeland.

It was discovered there in 1921 and spawned what was surely the first new mining industry of post-independence Ireland, with extraction beginning even as a certain ill-fated Treaty was being debated in the Dáil.

Jamesie's job seemed very glamorous to us as children, involving as it did long daily trips to such mysterious foreign parts as Waterford and Kerry. We often had to wait late into the night for him to return from these semi-legendary travels. But we kept the vigils faithfully, because wherever he was coming from, he always brought sweets home.

I can still hear Auntie Mary commanding silence in the kitchen – 'Whisht!' – as the sound of a car would be heard in the distance. We would then listen in suspense to the gear changes, as the vehicle turned corners and climbed hills.

Sometimes it was a false alarm: the car would turn into another lane ('that's White's', or 'that's McCabe's', Auntie Mary would say). Or sometimes it would be a mysterious stranger who just kept going past our lane, driving to God knows where. But our hero would return eventually, with a bag of Oatfield Emeralds or some other treasure, and great always was the rejoicing.

Jamesie had his eccentric side too. He enjoyed, for example, scaring the bejayzus out of us occasionally, for no good reason. A running tease of his concerned their sitting room (aka 'the Room'), which was always locked and off limits to us. This was probably just a more extreme version of the policy whereby 'the Room' was reserved for special visitors.

But whenever we asked why, Jamesie liked to hint that something sinister had happened in there once, and that there was a ghost now that needed confining. Naturally, this helped us sleep well at night, especially when we were in the bedroom just above.

Jamesie sometimes regretted not having joined his brothers, who had all emigrated to Chicago (or 'Chicargo', as we always pronounced it). I can still see him taking a long drag of a cigarette in conversations with my father, staring into the middle distance, and saying: 'That was my big mistake. Not going to America.'

I don't think he ever got there, even as a holiday. Alas, he died in the 1980s, soon after retiring from the Gyp. Auntie Mary outlived him by a quarter of a century, reaching her nineties, a spartan to the end.

There was a row of fir trees on the hill behind their house, through which the wind whistled on dark January nights. I always think of Auntie Mary now as being like one of those firs: narrow, angular and upright.

The trees are still there, as I noticed on a drive past recently. But beyond them, on another exposed ridge, there was now a row of wind turbines, weirdly majestic, harvesting the breeze.

Even more strange, in a place we once considered so

remote, was the big garden centre and café just down the road from Auntie Mary's old house. It would have been unimaginable to us as children, exiled in East Cavan Siberia. But it was as busy as the windmills the day I dropped in, proving again the rule: build it and they will come.

***

Speaking of gypsum, at the age of seven I was to have an intimate acquaintance with one of its by-products: plaster of Paris. In school one day, I fell over and broke my leg. The actual accident and most of the subsequent visits to Monaghan General Hospital are now lost to memory.

But I'll never forget the strange experience of having the injured limb wrapped in what looked like a roll of thick, wet toilet paper that quickly hardened into a shell. Nor will I forget one of the side effects of the plaster's bone-setting powers: the maddening itch that accompanied it, about which you could do nothing. My leg was a prisoner for six weeks. It was a Parisian liberation the day the plaster came off again.

Mind you, the soft bandaging had to come off too, which even on a seven-year-old leg involved the yanking of a lot of small hairs. I remember that operation as well, with some trauma. It was carried out by our local doctor, Rory O'Hanlon (a future Minister for Health and father of Ardal). Apparently, I squealed like one of those castrated piglets mentioned earlier.

Plaster of Paris is so called because that city used to have a lot of gypsum under it. So extensive was the mining there at one time that there have been many street collapses over the centuries, as buildings fell into the hollowed-out ground. The bone-filled Catacombs, now a macabre tourist attraction, are among the subterranean spaces left by mining.

While visiting Paris in 2011, I wrote about the history of gypsum there for my *Irish Times* column, playing up the little-known link between Montparnasse and Magheracloone. The comparison turned out to be more apt than I realised. A few years later, a large sinkhole opened in one of the Magheracloone Mitchells' GAA club pitches, the result of a century of mining. The whole club had to be relocated.

***

A sports ground closer to home was the Carrick Rovers soccer pitch, which from the early 1970s onwards was next door to our house, on the other side of the cow-byre and the field behind us.

The frequency with which balls were kicked into our field during games led to the club asking permission to build a wooden stile in the hedgerow, for quicker retrievals. This carried the perk for us of free admission to all matches, saving us the modest entry fee levelled on those who had to enter via the main gate.

The nearest thing to glamour games at the time were during the annual Stedfast Cup, named for a local shoe factory, which pitted together teams from all over Cavan and Monaghan. The biggest draw was when Carrick played the mighty Tunney Meat Packers from Clones, the Real Madrid of amateur football in the northeast then, before near-capacity attendances of 250.

Then one day, many years later, Jack Charlton's

Republic of Ireland played there, and several thousand people came to watch, or tried to. It was the build-up to Ireland's World Cup qualifiers in 1993. And the bizarre turn of events arose because, needing a base not far from Dublin that also offered good fishing and golf, the team had chosen Carrick's Nuremore Hotel.

The local soccer club then offered their pitch for training and were surprised when the offer was accepted. They also offered to have it rolled first, to minimise the undulations of a field that one unkind Dublin newspaper said had 'more folds than an unmade bed'.

But Ireland were preparing for games away to Latvia and Lithuania, whose pitches were not exactly bowling lawns either. The poor condition of the Carrick Rovers pitch was ideal, apparently. Under Jack Charlton's game plan, the ball didn't spend much time on the ground anyway.

For the several days his team played beside our cowhouse, attendance records were obliterated. There were serious traffic jams outside and players ran the gauntlet of every autograph hunter in the northeast. Eventually, training sessions had to be relocated to Oriel Park in Dundalk, which was somewhat better adapted to dealing with crowds.

I was working in Dublin at the time, as a freelance journalist. Hearing of the chaos, however, I had to come home and witness one of the training sessions in person.

The word 'surreal' is overused these days. But I think it applies to the occasion on which, bypassing the security cordon at the pitch entrance, I climbed up on the roof of one of our outhouses and from there stepped onto the roof of the Carrick Rovers dressing room, where a photographer from *The Irish Times* (a paper I didn't work for yet) had his zoom lens trained on Roy Keane.

A reporter from *The Irish Independent* was sniffy – literally – about the choice of venue, complaining of the 'rural smells' to which refined urban noses were exposed that week: from our farm, presumably. I never heard what Roy thought of preparing for World Cup '94 in the field beside our cowshed. But eight years later, I wondered if the road to Saipan had started from there.

View from the Gods
6 August 2021

I TOOK A BOOK DOWN from the shelf the other day and a forgotten photograph fell out. It was a bird's eye view of the house I grew up in, captured by one of those small planes that used to tour the country for this purpose prior to a follow-up visit by a salesman selling the results.

If I had forgotten the photo, the moment it was taken remained a vivid memory, even though it was in the early 1970s. You wouldn't know unless you'd been there, but I'm in the picture, alongside my younger brother, squinting up at the plane. We had been hoeing weeds along the garden wall, following an extensive campaign of nagging from our mother.

I can't put a year on the scene now, but the season is autumn, clearly. The hayshed is full. Recently lifted haycocks have left circles in the grass of a neighbour's field. Adjoining that, a crop of barley ripens in what later became a soccer pitch: a pitch that, in a then unimaginable future, would one day host Jack Charlton's Republic of Ireland team for a World Cup training camp.

The aerial view does not do justice to our orchard, long since vanished. I remember it as a magical place, full of old trees with different personalities and names, including 'Beauty of Bath'. It looks a bit dishevelled in the picture, an undistinguished muddle of greenery. But the giant beeches opposite the house look just as majestic as they seemed.

Not that my mother ever appreciated their grandeur. She was too busy worrying about them falling some windy night and causing an accident. She worried a lot about the road, with good reason, having seven children. Irish roads were perilous in the 1970s, as an ever-increasing number of cars poured onto them without the improved driving standards or policing to match.

The photograph also brings back tragedies involving friends and neighbours, and one in particular that happened nearby. But we were lucky.

Our yard had a slight drop towards the gate, which reminds me of two contrasting car-related incidents from my teenage years.

Once I arrived home to find my father, mother and two siblings trying to push our Ford Escort up the yard, and struggling. I joined in, and the extra weight made all the difference. The car shot ahead, almost comically.

My mother laughed with pride at having raised such a strapping son. 'You'd know you were there,' she said. I had announced my manhood. But then, one day not long afterwards, and less admirably, I also propelled the car in the opposite direction.

It was an early driving lesson (unaccompanied) and, for reasons that remain unclear, I failed to engage the brake. Instead, the car glided out the gate and across the two-lane road, where I turned it smoothly and came to a halt, using natural gravity.

After noting with interest that I was still alive, my second emotion was embarrassment. Realising that family members had been watching, I hoped it looked deliberate and pretended accordingly.

My dog Rover was less fortunate. It is a lingering regret, still, that I inflicted such a clichéd name upon him. A loveable, eccentric, half black labrador, half red setter, he deserved something more distinctive.

But one day after I turned 18, my mother entered in a panic to say he had just been hit by a car. It wasn't the dog she was worried about for the moment, it was the possible court case. Like many of her generation, I suspect she was haunted by the thought that we were only one or two bad moves away from ruin. This might be the start of it.

My father was out in the fields somewhere, so it fell to me to go and face the man. It was a long walk. The dog had fled the scene but there was a big, Rover-shaped dent in the bumper of a parked Audi, and a small pool of blood in front of it.

The driver stood alongside, waiting. 'Sorry about your dog,' he said. I shrugged to say these things happen, then heard myself ask: 'What about your car?' I had no idea where the rest of that conversation might go. But the man just said: 'Don't worry about the car.'

Rover had limped into the front shed, where he was breathing his last painfully on a damp clay floor I can still smell. I wished we still had our old shotgun, not that I would have known how to use it.

Then he died quietly anyway. I put him in an empty 10-10-20 fertiliser bag and carried him with a spade over to the fairy fort in the field opposite. It felt a bit like burying childhood. A week later, I left to start work in Dublin.

The Longest Hay Day

THE SUMMER I WAS 10, my father fell ill – it was something called pericarditis, an inflammation of the membrane around the heart – and spent three months in hospital.

There was never a good time for a farmer to be sick back then, but haymaking season was the worst. We had to throw ourselves on the mercy of relatives and friends that year. Happily, the weather proved merciful too. The hay was cut, dried and baled in quick order. It only remained then for it to be drawn in from the fields. But that was the problem.

There were two routes to where the hay bales were. One was a long, winding lane – the official right of way that had come with the 30-acre farm my father bought just before I was born. Unfortunately, near the end of that lane lived a man we called 'Pipes' – long dead now – who had retrospectively objected to the purchase, and the right of way that went with it.

I don't know where the name 'Pipes' derived: yes, he smoked one, but so did my father and many men then. It may have been an inherited nickname, immortalising some incident or idiosyncrasy in family history. In any case, he and my father had been good friends once. Then, as so often happened in Ireland, a row over land intervened.

Buying the farm doubled our holding to 60 acres: hardly ranch-like, even by Monaghan standards, but enough to cause resentment for some in an era when inherited memories of the Land War still lingered.

Had the farm gone unsold, it might have been acquired by the Land Commission, a government body set up in

29

the nineteenth century by the British government but still active in the early decades of Irish independence, mostly in the redistribution of big, broken-up estates.

The commission tended to favour young farmers with families, whereas Pipes was a bachelor of late middle age. Nevertheless, feeling himself cheated by the sale of a possible windfall, he had ever since been on a revenge mission against us: a one-man agrarian terror campaign.

There were many guerrilla tactics in his repertoire. They ranged from opening gates at night, maliciously, so that cows would wander astray, to sabotaging farm machinery by throwing rocks and other objects into crops.

He liked to burn things too: typically hedgerows and other vegetation. Once, as a seven-year-old sent to bed early, I struggled to sleep because of a small fire in the orchard, visible from the bedroom window. Our pyromaniac neighbour had become such a bogeyman by then, I thought it must be him, as I told my mother on a tearful visit down to the kitchen. Only when assured that it was just my father burning weeds could I go back to sleep.

But one of the most effective tactics in our enemy's repertoire involved planting six-inch nails in the lane: hammered through thin slats of wood and then buried, pointing upwards, in such a way as to pierce any tractor tyre that crossed them.

He was so adept at this that my father quickly abandoned the right of way in favour of a plan B. When another adjoining property came up for sale, the purchaser agreed – in return for a free run at it – to sell us a small strip on the periphery that would connect the two parts of our farm.

The downside of this new lane was that getting to it involved a diagonal crossing of the steep hill behind our house. That was a typical Monaghan drumlin and would be no obstacle to today's powerful tractors. But it was dangerous then, especially if you had a heavily laden trailer behind.

Even so, my father learned how to negotiate this north-west passage safely, using low second gear and with the added assistance of the Rosaries my mother would always be saying at the time. Somehow, he never overturned.

My mother's confidence in the power of prayer did not, however, extend to third parties. There could be no question of us asking strangers to risk the hill.

So with my father languishing in hospital that summer, an emergency summit of the extended family was held, and a fateful decision taken. We would mount a mass land-and-air assault on the lane. Well, land mostly.

I'll never forget the dawn of that momentous day. It was our version of the Normandy landings, as a never-before-seen force of seven tractors and trailers, driven by uncles and neighbours, departed our back yard.

I don't remember us calling the Belmullet weather station the night before to check on possible Atlantic weather systems that might threaten the operation. Otherwise, nothing was left to chance.

Being 10, I was too young to drive a tractor myself. Under the health and safety regulations of the time, you had to be at least 11 before they'd let you do that. Instead, as acting man of the house, I was posted on sentry duty outside the nail-layer's den, lest he emerge during lulls in traffic to strike again.

I was of course petrified. Even with so many tractors, there were long gaps between hay-loads when the loneliness of a dark country lane was unnerving. I had no idea what to do if the enemy appeared – was I supposed to fight him?

He must have been pushing 60 by that time. And, God love him, he was probably even more nervous at the dramatic events unfolding than I was. In any case, he didn't stir from his house all day.

***

Looking back, I have only pity for him now. He was a product of his time and circumstances, when one man's victory in land, however small, was another's defeat.

Also looking back, I don't know why we didn't just get a metal detector and sweep the lane for nails. Perhaps such inventions hadn't yet impinged on our consciousness back then. Anyway, like most of Pipes's one-man land war, the nail campaign petered out soon afterwards.

Mind you, at its height, it had also seen a friendly fire incident involving his own family. He himself always travelled by bicycle – he had no car or tractor and so was at little risk of self-inflicted punctures. Besides, he knew where the nails were buried.

He also lived alone. But he had a half-forgotten sister in America, who had emigrated years before. And one day, she paid him a surprise visit, in a rental vehicle presumably, suffering one or more flat tyres in the process.

It was a rude welcome home, made worse by the fact that her brother was out at the time. She called in to my parents – old friends of hers too – afterwards, mystified, and was filled in on the sad turn of events.

***

It must have been sometime after D-Day that I launched my own counter-terror campaign against the nail man.

One morning, on an emboldened whim, as he cycled past me on the road into town, I coughed sarcastically.

Maybe the first time this happened, he thought I had a cold. But by the second or third occasion, he knew it was deliberate. Then I did it once too often. And instead of just cycling on, that time, he turned the bike around.

This seemed to happen in slow motion. So did the freezing of my blood, which accompanied it. In 10 years of existence, I had never met the bogeyman face to face before, or heard his voice. Now, thanks to my coughing campaign, I was about to experience both. The result was dumbfounding. All sarcasm, not to mention courage, deserted me. I stood, frozen to the spot, in silence.

Most of his verbal tirade is now lost to memory, perhaps buried by the ensuing post-traumatic stress disorder. I do, however, still clearly recall one of the things he called me: 'You crooked-eyed little cunt!'

The phrase may have appealed to him only for its alliterative and rhythmic qualities – it certainly rolls off the tongue. But as I recovered from the shock in subsequent days, I did find myself sneaking looks at the mirror, wondering if my eyes were in fact misaligned.

Another subsequent trauma was having to repeat the details to my parents. First, one of my older sisters, Majella, debriefed me on the incident. Then she relayed a summary to my father – by now back in harness – who in turn cross-examined me at length.

'And what else did he call you?' he asked finally, knowing I was holding back something. I swallowed hard. 'A crooked-eyed little c...,' I said, choking on the last word.

After that, there was an unmistakeable sense that my coughing, and the reaction it provoked, had escalated the war. Sure enough, one subsequent evening, I noticed both my parents lingering in the vicinity of our front gate, stealing occasional looks down the road, whence the enemy was expected to appear imminently on his way into town.

He must have seen the ambush coming, because, a man of few words normally, he stopped on the way for an inordinately long chat with a neighbour who was mowing the lawn. Then he reluctantly accepted his fate and, as he took to his bike again and passed our house, my parents struck.

The attack was purely verbal, with no bad language – or at least none that could be heard from the safe distance behind the frontline, where I was lurking. But it was the first time I had ever heard these former friends exchange words. The effect was almost as electrifying as the hay-day landings.

Snippets of the angry conversation floated on the breeze. I heard Pipes protest at the outrage whereby 'decent people' couldn't travel the road with being 'abused', while my parents countered that I was 'only a child' and he should be 'ashamed' of himself.

In general, it was his turn to be cowed. My parents did most of the talking, although the only sentence I recall in full was my mother's parting shot: 'And there's nothing wrong with his eyes!' Somehow, this did not reassure me. I was still checking the mirror for a good while afterwards.

An instructive aspect of the affair was that my father never gave out to me for my part in it, exactly. He suggested only that I had picked the wrong target.

It was long acknowledged in our house that, much as he had aggrieved us, Pipes was not the worst party to the dispute. That role was attributed to another neighbour, also now long dead, who we suspected had provoked the whole thing while never getting his own hands dirty.

'You can cough at him all you like,' my father told me. For various reasons, I never acted on that advice, and instead retired from throat-clearing vigilantism with immediate effect.

***

By a sad coincidence, many years later, when my father was dying, he and his estranged former friend found themselves in the same hospital, simultaneously. Pipes was in the marginally better condition of the two: his stay that time was only temporary. My father meanwhile, was bed-bound.

So before Pipes was released, my mother sought him out and, committed Christian that she was, suggested he pay a final visit to his neighbour and make peace before it was too late. And fair play to him, he did, telling my father he would say a prayer for him. They were both dead by autumn.

Local land disputes like this were common in most parts of Ireland once. John B. Keane's *The Field* dramatised an extreme example, including murder, in Kerry. As filmed by Jim Sheridan, that became a sort of Shakespearean tragedy.

Our South Monaghan version of the genre had even inspired poetry on occasion. Recalling from his youth a mere boundary dispute between Inniskeen neighbours, Patrick Kavanagh wrote the sonnet 'Epic', in which he compares the incident with Greek mythology, via Homer: 'I made the *Iliad* from such / A local row.'

So I plead literary licence for likening our little drama

to D-Day. In any case, Operation Haymaker was a huge success. By nightfall, the hayshed was full for another winter. But it had come at a cost. We were also mourning the poor Fordson, which lay grievously wounded, with four flat tyres.

It had done its job heroically. Only one of our neighbours also suffered a puncture – and refused our offers to pay for the repair. My uncle Frank, meanwhile, had acquired a ticket from a passing garda for some technical infringement during the part of the operation that involved the main road. There were no other casualties.

Our Fordson Dexta was succeeded a year or two later by a Massey Ferguson 165. I don't know what happened to it after that. Perhaps its remains are still mouldering today somewhere, forgotten, in a Tomb of the Unknown Tractor.

A Proustian Moment: In Search of Lost Hay Bales

17 June 2011

A PRESS RELEASE JUST ARRIVED from the Trim Haymaking Festival – which, incorporating the 'Scurlogstown Olympiad', takes place this Sunday – and with it a vanished world came back to life.

Excuse me while I have a Proustian moment here. But was ever so much lost in the name of progress as in the decline of hay in Ireland and its replacement by that unloved winter fodder: silage?

Perhaps this is unfair. Silage-making may have its charms too, for all I know. No doubt you can learn to love the smell of molasses, or lactic acid bacteria, being added to new-cut grass.

The midwinter aroma of a fermenting pit probably also has its fans. All I know is that the smells of hay-making, inhaled in childhood, stay with you forever.

Smells aside, the work had a ritual aspect that, pleasantly protracted, seemed part of the natural order. It lasted as long the traditional wake – three to four days. And, if the weather stayed fine, it could be just as enjoyable.

First the hay had to be cut; then allowed to dry where it fell; then turned at least once to dry some more, before being cocked or baled; and finally, in triumph, brought home.

The last bit was the best. Among the many now-useless skills I learned as a child is that neglected branch of architecture: the 'building' of hay-loads. Which, once built, became your transport for the homeward journey.

There can be no more luxurious trip anywhere than

sitting or lying (as with all high-end travel, the seat easily extended into a bed) on a load of bales being drawn home by tractor and trailer through the fields.

It had its dangers, occasionally. You could be wiped off the top by a low-lying branch, for example. Or you could get a smack in the face from a branch bent out of the way by a passenger in front and then released too suddenly, by accident or design.

I was also one of several small passengers on the top deck once when, going down the side of a hill, the trailer 'coped'.

I don't know even now where that verb came from: in the meaning we used it – 'to overturn' – no English dictionary can enlighten me. Also, in the commonly understood sense of the word, coping is exactly what the trailer failed to do on this occasion.

But the main thing is that we coped too, in both the term's meanings. As the load began to tilt, we scrambled onto the high side. And as soon as it went over, so did we. It only added to the day's fun.

Unfortunately, the protracted nature of hay-making was also part of its downside. It required three or four consecutive days without rain: freak conditions in most Irish summers. If you mistimed the cutting, it could be lying in the fields for weeks, being turned again and again and then soaked anew.

Or worse, panicked by a forecast, you might bale before it was dry enough, in which case you could look forward to a rotting smell soon rising from the hayshed, like blight in the potato field.

Still, there was great satisfaction when the job ended successfully. I like the Old Testament resonance of the idea that hay was something to be 'saved'.

Whereas, in keeping with the soulless nature of the operation, nobody ever speaks of saving silage. Nor indeed – leaving religion out of it a moment – does one now hear of couples 'rolling in the silage', no matter how hot the weather.

There were other things lost too. The communal nature of hay-making, for example. Farmers used to have to help each other out with it and the rhythms of the work allowed for plenty of talk-time. That all went with silage harvesting, where machinery – the bigger and faster, the better – eliminated human interaction.

Wildlife suffered too. Bumblebees and butterflies declined in parallel with hay-making. So did certain kinds of birds, most famously corncrakes. Preferring their vegetation to be more than 20cm high, these shy creatures did not adapt well to silage, which is cut earlier and more often than hay, blowing their cover.

Then there were the new things that, along with increased efficiency, silage brought. Slurry, for one. I won't go into details in case you're having breakfast. Suffice to say that cattle slurry as we know it is a modern development, arising as it did from the change to a silage diet.

That the new-style effluent is in turn ideally suited to be recycled as fertiliser is part of its efficiency. But I have yet to hear even the most hardcore farmer wax lyrical about the smell of slurry, compared with which old-style manure was like vintage Armagnac.*

---

* Having said all that, in the interests of balance, I should record what a Cavan letter-writer named Brendan Dunleavy said after I waxed nostalgic about hay-making. He was among those who first introduced the big round silage bales to Ireland, circa 1980. And one of his motivations, he told me,

Oh well. It's all part of the price of scientific advance, which marches ever onwards. In the meantime, veteran haymakers can at least wallow in nostalgia occasionally at the likes of this weekend's event (see trimhaymaking festival.com). And nostalgia aside, as the subtitle implies, the festival also has a strong sporting element, with competitive disciplines to include 'scythe-cutting', 'sheaf-tossing' and the inaugural 'cic ard' contest.

That last one, in case you're wondering, involves no agricultural equipment. Meath footballer Graham Geraghty and others will merely compete to kick a ball over a 90ft-high bar. But then again, the boundaries between GAA and agriculture are easily confused, especially at this time of year. The Trim event takes place a week before the eagerly awaited Louth–Meath rematch. It would be no surprise if the odd haymaker featured there too.

---

was 'farmer's lung'. This was a disease caused by the dust in the old, small square bales, which 'polluted the air in hay-sheds with millions of fungal spores'. The result had shortened thousands of lives, and there was and remains no cure. 'So by all means let us remember the square hay bale with nostalgia,' Brendan wrote, 'but not with regret at its demise.'

Caught in a Cross Fire

ACROSS THE FIELDS FROM WHERE I grew up, there was a small limestone quarry from which explosions were occasionally heard.

It was owned by a man named Jack McCabe, who also owned the first mechanical diggers I ever saw. In my childhood world, the letters JCB stood for 'Jack McCabe's Bulldozers'. It was a big disappointment when I first realised that the acronym referred instead to a giant machinery plant in England.

But whenever a bang was heard from the direction of the quarry in the early 1970s, there was always a possible alternative explanation. I recall a neighbour dropping in one day and, at the sound of a dull thud somewhere behind him, wondering: 'Is that McCabe's or Crossmaglen?'

Crossmaglen was a small town 10 miles to the northeast, just across the border in Northern Ireland. And to this day, I can't honestly say whether the sound of explosions there would have carried across that distance, and the many drumlins in between – especially considering that the prevailing winds tend to blow the other way.

In any case, Crossmaglen loomed large in our imaginations then, as it did increasingly in the minds of people as far away as London's Downing Street. It was the heart of Republican South Armagh: a very dangerous place for British soldiers, soon to be dubbed by Northern Secretary Merlyn Rees – in a nickname that has stuck ever since – 'Bandit Country'.

In the 30 years of Northern Ireland's 'Troubles', at least 58 policemen and twice as many troops were killed in the area. At the time it was considered the most hazardous posting anywhere in the world for a British soldier. Road patrols being so prone to ambush, a nearby army helicopter base was said to be the busiest in Europe.

Years later, working my way around Australia in 1989, I briefly roomed with a young ex-army Scotsman who had been posted to the barracks in Crossmaglen for six months and was somewhat traumatised by the experience.

There was a lot of confined-to-barracks boredom, he said, but one day a colleague put his hand over a parapet and had the top of a finger shot off. Back home afterwards and threatened with another trip to South Armagh, my Scots friend had opted for a return to civilian life.

While our local town – Carrickmacross – was called 'Carrick' for short, Crossmaglen was always abbreviated to 'Cross'. This seemed apt in more ways than one. Although 'the Troubles' was itself a euphemism for Ireland's twentieth-century wars, I have read somewhere that it was pre-dated for a while during the War of Independence by 'the Crossness', which now sounds almost polite.

That had nothing to do with South Armagh, as such. But 'Cross' did seem a very angry place in the 1970s and 1980s. Locals' relationship with the security forces was epitomised by a sculpture in the town square of an unarmed but defiant man, fists clenched, squaring up to an unseen oppressor.

Similarity of names aside, Carrick and Cross were also linked by a narrow, winding road and a certain shared notoriety. After the border descended on the area in the early 1920s, the route became 'unapproved', meaning there was no permanent checkpoint on it, and so making it popular with smugglers, who would take their chances with mobile customs checks.

Even before it became an international frontier, however, and perhaps dating back to a time when this was a buffer zone between the Dublin Pale and the Gaelic north, the area was associated with what might be termed sharp business practices, legal and otherwise. In Carrick, we would usually blame the resultant reputation mainly on Cross, but like the road, the notoriety was two-way.

There is a well-known comic ballad, popularised by Tommy Makem, about a man from those parts who is arrested for being drunk and disorderly. The chorus summarises his plea of innocence as follows: 'It wasn't the boys from Shercock or the lads from Ballybay / Twas the dealin' men from Crossmaglen put whiskey in me tay.'

Another verse includes the line – as pleaded by the accused: 'From Carrickmacross to Crossmaglen, as any man will vow / There are no rogues but honest men for miles and miles around.' But this claim would probably have sounded like an overreach at the best of times, never mind as a defence strategy in a court case. In any event, as often happens to famous quotations that were not completely convincing in the original, posterity has rewritten it. Now, whenever people quote the lines, they usually reverse the Makem version, i.e. 'From Carrickmacross to Crossmaglen, there *are* more rogues than honest men.'

As a child in the mid-1970s, I felt vaguely implicated in the area's shady reputation, being an occasional accomplice then in a minor cross-border butter-importation racket run by a gang whose leaders were my parents. The operation involved us driving the six and a half miles to South Armagh and then down a narrow side road, where there was a grocery shop called Paddy Larry's. There we would buy a box of butter – 24 pounds of it – and very little else, as I remember, before fleeing back across the border.

The butter was for personal use. There were seven children in our family; a box probably kept us going for a month at the most. And besides, nearly everybody was at it then. There would have been butter-related tailbacks – butter jams, if you like – at the border at the time, except that not everybody had a car.

Where cars were lacking, others took up the slack. I remember a school-bus driver who ran a popular local service distributing boxes of Northern butter as well as students. It was the sort of lesson in hard economics they didn't teach you at school.

There was nothing illegal about our butter buying – it just felt like smuggling. But in some places the widespread cross-border trade was considered unpatriotic. Questions were asked about it in the Dáil and the government took a dim view.

I can't remember wrestling, as a 10-year-old, with the ethical issues involved, including whether my father, as a dairy farmer and Fianna Fáil councillor, should buy butter anywhere except in the local jurisdiction. But if I had done, I probably would have pleaded political motivation. Even as moderate nationalists, we resented the border. We had never asked for it. It was imposed by others, cutting us off from a natural hinterland.

Furthermore, we knew that the 1924 Boundary Commission, which would probably have liberated Paddy Larry's, at least, had been a political stitch-up from the start. I wrote about Paddy Larry's in my *Irish Times* column decades later, when the high price of butter in the Republic was again a cause of controversy.

An interesting footnote to that was an email from a

man in Donegal who had married a native of the area. He astounded me by suggesting that Paddy Larry's had been in Monaghan all along, which – if true – meant that, on those supposed cross-border trips, we had never left the Republic.

Further enquiries have since established the possibility that Paddy may have had two shops, close together but on either side of the border. Or maybe it was one shop that straddled the two jurisdictions. I still don't know. All I can say for certain is that, wherever the shop we bought our butter was, the British Labour government's cheap food policies extended there.

The odd bang from across the fields apart, Carrick was a much quieter place during the 1970s and 1980s than Cross. The Troubles seemed a safe distance away from us, most of the time.

But the muffled explosions from Crossmaglen – real or imagined – now seem like a metaphor too. Ireland in general was a dangerous country then. And every so often, suddenly, the noises of war got nearer.

One ominous day at school, in the mid-1970s, a few of us were testing each other's reflexes by throwing a tennis ball around the classroom, hard and with surprise changes of direction, like a more violent version of 'Tig'.

When one of the boys – Gerard Martin – missed a catch, the ball hit him squarely on the ear. In the short term, it just hurt. But afterwards, at home, he became unwell. His alarmed parents brought him to the doctor, who recommended they drive him to the Eye and Ear Hospital in Dublin for a check-up, just in case.

An hour or two later, somewhere on the outskirts of the capital, they heard a boom in the background. It was 17 May 1974. While the Martins were caught up in their own little emergency that day, three car bombs went off in Dublin and another in Monaghan town, killing 35 people. The cars had come from North Armagh – taking revenge on innocents for the activities of republicans in Crossmaglen and elsewhere. British army involvement was rumoured, and still is.

But even that horror did not directly impinge on Carrick. Monaghan town was almost 30 miles north of us. The slaughter there seemed almost as distant as Dublin's. Maybe we were more nervous of parked cars than before: a common condition by then on both sides of the Irish Sea.

Otherwise, life went on as usual. Our town was busy enough that not even the most cliché-addicted journalist, reporting violent events there, would describe it as 'normally sleepy'. And it did serve as a frontier posting, so that to this day I regularly meet people from other parts of Ireland whose knowledge of Carrick dates from a period in the 1970s or 1980s, when their fathers were gardaí there.

Still, it felt safe most of the time. Hence the shock one day when a soldier dismounting from a jeep outside the Garda barracks accidentally fired a round from an Uzi submachine gun through the window of a car and nearly killed a neighbour of ours.

Mrs Bridgy McNally (no relation) had been sitting quietly in the passenger seat when a bullet grazed her head. After having the wound dressed by a local GP, she was sent home with little fuss. There was no post-traumatic stress counselling in those days.

The army had been in town to guard a cash shipment in the local AIB. And the accident could have happened anywhere in Ireland then, because bank robberies (usually as fundraisers for republican groups) were ubiquitous. Even so, it seemed like a local detour of the Troubles raging a few miles away.

Then there was August 1979, when the deadliest day of the IRA's campaign carried local reverberations, although the events again seemed distant from us. There were two attacks: one 25 miles east of Carrickmacross, at Warrenpoint, well beyond earshot, although it involved a pair of massive explosions that between them killed 18 members of Britain's parachute regiment.

The other incident was in the far northwest, at Mullaghmore Bay in Sligo, where a bomb obliterated a boat carrying Lord Louis Mountbatten, uncle of Britain's then future King Charles. The assassination of such a senior member of royalty (and three unlucky civilians, two of them teenage boys) overshadowed the IRA's other ambush that day, making news headlines all over the world.

And it soon emerged that it was a Carrickmacross man who had planted the device. Thomas McMahon, known to most of us as a carpenter until then, had also been one of the IRA's most experienced bomb-makers. Now, suddenly, his name was internationally infamous.

McMahon was arrested at a routine Garda checkpoint as he left the scene in Sligo, even before the explosion went off. He served 17 years for the murders before being released under the Good Friday Agreement amnesty.

It was reported that he had cut his links with militant republicanism, although years later, back in 'Cross' as an *Irish Times* reporter, I watched him lay the wreath at an annual commemoration for two other IRA bombers, Brendan Moley and Brendan Burns, killed by one of their own devices in 1988.

I had left school the year of the Warrenpoint and Sligo ambushes and got my first proper summer job in the tile factory just across the road from where we lived. The day after the attacks, one of my older colleagues there, a hardline republican, exulted in the IRA's triumphs, making childishly bad jokes about what the scene must have looked like and mocking my teenage sensitivity at the horror.

Soon afterwards, I was applying for permanent jobs, increasingly scarce by then in a Republic heading for the deepest recession in decades. One of the things I nearly did was become a garda: state security being a rare employment growth area at the time.

I didn't pursue that in the end. But a friend from school – Gary Sheehan – did, with tragic results. He became the first victim of the Troubles that I knew personally. And it was through him that the brutal reality of the war raging a few miles to the north of us was finally brought home, even to the usually peaceful Carrickmacross. But we'll come back to that.

Leonid Brezhnev:
My Part in his Downfall

As the Cold War reached a dangerous new phase in the late 1970s, a fixture of my year was the annual Civil Defence seminar, in which leaders of the community were trained to monitor local radiation levels during the nuclear winter we were expecting any day soon.

My father was the nearest thing to a community leader in our house. But by then, only at gunpoint could he have been persuaded to spend a day sitting in a classroom, listening to lectures. So with the qualities that made him a leader, he always delegated his nuclear disaster training to me.

The working assumption at the seminars was that Ireland would not be attacked directly. The bad news was that we were in the flight path of the intercontinental ballistic missiles, so unplanned stopovers at Shannon and elsewhere could not be ruled out.

Windscale (as it still was then, soon to be renamed Sellafield), located directly across the water from us in Cumbria, was a potential target too. Wherever the bombs fell, though, nowhere would be safe from the red dust.

It wouldn't be red in real life, of course, only in the little line drawings that illustrated the Civil Defence manual, a cheap production even by the standards of the time.

In the drawings, the civilian population was portrayed safely indoors, sitting in the most central room of each house – the 'refuge room' – while outside, red dust gathered on the sandbags they had piled against the walls before retreating.

In practice, the dust would be an invisible enemy. 'It cannot be seen or felt,' warned the manual, 'but we have instruments to tell us when it is about.' This is where the community leaders came in, though I remember thinking that if the manual was a guide to the quality of our instruments, we were all in trouble.

Our local seminar was held in a place that, were it ever the scene of a major news story, would be described by journalists as 'the normally sleepy town of Ballybay'.

Chosen for its centrality, Ballybay was the refuge room of County Monaghan. Not to exaggerate how quiet it could be, suffice to say that on a wet weekday in the 1970s, it was as good a place as any to contemplate the prospect of a post-nuclear wasteland.

Community leaders aside, the Civil Defence plan was heavily dependent on Radio Éireann, as it was still known. In the event of an emergency, the booklet said, the station would broadcast official warnings. There would be an advance warning one hour before the fallout reached Ireland, and after that a final warning to say the fallout had descended.

Then it would be time for the community leaders to spring into action, making short forays outside with our Geiger counters, measuring radiation levels in selected spots, and pausing only to shoot looters.

OK, I made the last bit up. We weren't that important: shooting looters would be somebody else's job. We were mere functionaries. Our role would be confined to relaying the readings to Dublin, assuming Dublin was still there.

Looking back now, I don't know how real the danger of a US–Soviet conflict was. But after the Nixon–Brezhnev détente of the early 1970s, the Cold War had hotted up again, with occasionally notorious incidents such as the

1978 assassination of a Bulgarian dissident in London by poison-tipped umbrella.

The conflict also extended to the airwaves, where the superpowers fought each other with propaganda. It was easier at the time to find communist brainwashing on the medium-wave dial than an Irish station playing pop records.

You didn't even need a radio. Around that time, I bought a second-hand electric guitar from part of the proceeds of my first proper summer job, working in the French-owned tile factory down the road.

The vendor was my school pal Breifne O'Rourke, a budding rock star who was trading up. For 40 quid, I secured his passable copy of a Fender Stratocaster and an amp. Which, between them, formed the basis of a doomed attempt to become the next Rory Gallagher.

The novelty soon wore off, even for me (it had worn off for my family somewhat earlier). By which time, all I had to show for it was a few isolated chords and the intro to The Ruts' angry punk hit 'Babylon's Burning'.

But the thing I'll always remember about the amp is that, perhaps because of some wiring repairs carried out by the previous owner, it also accidentally functioned as a shortwave radio receiver.

There was no tuning dial, so it only ever picked up one station. Whenever I turned it on at night, I often found myself listening to the world service from Radio Moscow. This was less unusual then than it seems now.

During the Leonid Brezhnev era, the Russians were well known for having very powerful transmitters pointed at the West, and for using multiple radio frequencies to get their message across. If you'd held up a pair of knitting needles at the time, you'd probably have intercepted one of the signals.

And yet for all the Soviet Union's efforts to infiltrate my amp and brainwash me, I struggle now to recall any of the programmes. My main memory is that, in common with most European radio presenters then, theirs had American accents.

Naturally, the news from Moscow did not dwell on shortcomings of the communist system. Or indeed on any unhappy events, unless they happened in America, or Britain, or in the 'police state' of Northern Ireland.

The latter, which was only a few miles from us (maybe that's why the signal was so good), featured a lot. Whereas, even after the Soviet invasion of Afghanistan, reports from Kabul would concentrate on such issues as the start of the 'spring sowing season'. The only hint of problems there might be occasional references to the obstruction of Afghan farmers by US-trained 'bandits'.

Speaking of police states, I've heard since of musicians occasionally picking up police radio broadcasts on their amps. If that had happened on mine, I might at least have learned useful information and maybe broken into the newspaper industry earlier. But it was only Radio Moscow I received, and I can't honestly say that was a good training in journalism.

In more paranoid moments, I sometimes wondered whether the amp might have a two-way link. If so, the repeated intros of 'Babylon's Burning' – a song about the terminal decay of Western society – may have encouraged false optimism among the eavesdroppers in the Kremlin. I just hope I didn't thereby prolong the suffering of the Russian people.

There was no escaping the great East–West conflict then. Another battleground was chess. That had come to a head in the autumn of 1978, with an epic world championship match that dragged on for four months.

The first player to reach six points would win; draws, of which there were many, didn't count. Amid allegations of spying, hypnotism and the covert use of colour-coded yoghurts, Anatoly Karpov eventually beat Viktor Korchnoi 6–5.

Both men were Russian, but Karpov was the Soviet poster boy while Korchnoi was a defector and darling of the West. They weren't just playing chess: they were fighting the Cold War by proxy.

So was I, second-hand. I used to follow the games avidly in the newspapers, sometimes playing out the moves on my chessboard in the kitchen late at night when I couldn't sleep.

The surrounding intrigue was often more exciting than the games themselves. One of the subplots involved a Soviet parapsychologist, Dr Zukhar, who sat in the front row and trained his kaleidoscope eyes on Korchnoi to put him off his game.

Korchnoi retaliated by hiring two American yogis, who in turn freaked out Zukhar by focusing their energies on him. Once, this caused him to cover his face with a handkerchief and leave the room. Mind you, the yogis were on bail after being accused of murdering an Indian diplomat, so it may have been more than yoga Zukhar was worried about.

Replaying the games at night was strangely relaxing. What with the stress of being a community leader, the looming apocalypse and 'Babylon Burning', I think I had insomnia for a while. Vicariously participating in a world championship chess match, even if it was a surrogate war, was light relief.

When not tuned in to Radio Moscow then, I was listening to Radio Caroline, a subversive experience in its own way. The station had been launched (literally – it was on a ship) back in the 1960s, aimed at circumventing the strict British broadcasting laws of the day, but with an Irish revolutionary subplot.

Its founder was a self-styled Dublin 'rebel', Ronan O'Rahilly, who had been expelled from school seven times before he gave it up at 17. He was a grandson of *The* O'Rahilly, who in 1916 – left out of the loop by the organisers – drove his luxury car from Kerry to the GPO to join the Easter Rising, and later died in a doorway off Moore Street, writing in a farewell note to his wife: 'It was a good fight anyway.'

Among other things, his family owned the small port of Greenore, 20-odd miles east of us in County Louth. And it was from there that Ronan O'Rahilly launched his smaller revolution in 1964, broadcasting pop music – then all but unknown on British and Irish airwaves – offshore.

By the time I first encountered Radio Caroline, pop music was readily available elsewhere, even in rural Monaghan, thanks to the invasion of our airwaves by BBC's new Radio 1 (joined, from 1979, by RTÉ's Radio 2). But Caroline had evolved into a station that played album music, something we would-be cool kids preferred to the terrible singles of the pre-punk hit parade.

I'll always remember the thrill of tuning in one night on my parents' old wooden-box 'wireless' and having my mind blown by a strange but wonderful song, the introduction to which had escaped me. Then I learned, even more thrillingly, that it was Pink Floyd: a band I had already decided to be a fan of, based on their name, hair length and album covers. The song was 'See Emily Play' – a single, ironically, from 1967, before its creators stopped making such things.

It started an intense adolescent love affair with the group, consummated mainly via Radio Caroline until I could afford to buy albums and play them secretly on my sister Anna's record player whenever she was out. This was a high-risk, covert activity. Discovery by the sister-hood's secret police could have had terrible consequences.

So in keeping with the general weirdness of the times, I used to listen to *Dark Side of the Moon* in my older sisters' bedroom, with the lights off, while sitting in the window to watch for signs of their return. When, in later years, I was able to play Pink Floyd records in fully lit rooms, without fear of discovery, it was never quite the same.

I don't remember there being ads on Radio Caroline. The only thing it seemed to be promoting was Eastern religion, one of O'Rahilly's other interests. There were regular spacey jingles that urged listeners to engage in 'loving awareness'. They didn't tell us how, but we did our best.

Maybe that contributed to the easing of international tensions too. In any case, the Cold War petered out harm-lessly enough in the end. I never did get my personal Geiger counter or have to worry about filling sandbags. And, like a lot of once-feared things that didn't happen, the temptation in retrospect is to think it was never likely in the first place, because there were too many sane people on both sides.

But a few years later, as we now know, there was something called the '1983 Soviet nuclear false alarm incident', which was not reported at the time or for many years afterwards. It occurred when, just after midnight on 26 September 1983, the USSR's computerised early-warning system signalled a launch by the US of several intercontinental ballistic missiles.

Luckily, a man named Stanislav Petrov, a Soviet air force officer on duty at the command centre where the warning was received, rightly suspected a false alarm and – in breach of orders – waited for more evidence before reporting it upwards to those who had fingers on buttons. No evidence emerged. Petrov thereby helped prevent a retaliation to the non-attack, which would likely have precipitated a retaliation to the retaliation, and maybe all-out war.

Of course, when none of that happened, the temptation again is to think it couldn't have, because of built-in safeguards. But that was a time of intense mutual suspicion between the superpowers and when the Soviet Union was crumbling dangerously, as Chernobyl soon demonstrated.

The 1983 incident was hushed up and Petrov's career did not thrive afterwards, because he had exposed uncomfortable truths. Now dead, he did at least live to see himself the hero of an award-winning Danish documentary in 2013. Made 30 years after the event and suggesting that some of us were closer than we ever realised to receiving Geiger counters in the post, it was called *The Man Who Saved the World*.

Getting back to my ambition to become a rock star, that crumbled a lot sooner than communism. It was around the same time that the US and Soviet Union began their Strategic Arms Reduction Talks (START), marking the beginning of the Cold War's end.

I like to believe that my eventual decision to decommission the amp was, in its own way, a small contribution to world peace. It was a contribution to peace in the McNally household anyway.

The threat of war had receded sufficiently by the mid-1980s that nuclear disaster training was no longer deemed necessary. Or maybe it was just that, given the state of the Irish economy at the time, the prospect of apocalypse was no longer as unattractive as it once seemed.

Whatever the reason, the local seminars stopped. A few years after that, the Berlin Wall came down and the Eastern Bloc welcomed a new era of democracy.

We couldn't have imagined it even then, but a decade on, instead of communist missiles, Monaghan was being targeted by post-communist migrants: thousands of them, from Latvia, Lithuania, Estonia, the Czech Republic and Poland, flocking to Celtic Tiger Ireland in search only of work.

Requiem for a Friend

IF OUR LEAVING CERT CLASS had had a 'boy most likely to succeed' award, it would have gone to Gary Sheehan. Certainly, he was the nearest thing some of us had to a role model. He was a year or more older than me, a big difference at that age. But he also had natural leadership qualities, which made him the obvious choice for class prefect.

Gary was an athlete as well, famously scoring two goals in the 1978 Monaghan minor county final in which Carrick Emmets lowered the colours of the mighty Castleblayney Faughs, an event then rare in the annals.

Most important, to me, he was popular with girls. He seemed to have everything they wanted. For those of us who had little of this mysterious quality, he was someone to watch and copy.

We were never best friends or anything like that. Although our homes were barely a mile apart on the same side of Carrickmacross, he was a townie and I, by virtue of growing up on a farm, was from 'the country'.

There was a subtle social divide, a farmer/cowboy thing. The townies could go to the Gaeltacht in summer, for example. We couldn't. Even so, Gary and I got on well and, for various reasons, he was present at several key moments of my life.

The only team sport medal I ever won was in a five-a-side soccer tournament in which he was our captain. We were also once members of the same Irish debating team (God knows why – my Irish was terrible, even then) that represented the Patrician Brothers High School against the local, vastly superior, St Louis Girls'.

They handed us our oratorical arses on a plate, of course. But Gary at least had the consolation of winning the best speaker award.

Crucially, too, he was in the near vicinity on the occasion that I first kissed a girl. I'll spare readers the full details, but for those under 50, I should explain that this was an earth-shattering event in the late 1970s: a bit like losing your virginity now, or something more serious.

Anyway, Gary was my cornerman then. As in the soccer tournament, he provided important advice on tactics, positioning, and when to strike.

I was a clueless 16-year-old when we did the Leaving Cert, so I repeated it, not picking up many clues the second time around. Gary repeated too, then got a job and left mid-year. The job was in Galway, where months later he would host a famous party the night before Pope John Paul II visited the city.

That was a never-to-be-forgotten weekend in Galway – not necessarily for reasons of which the pope might have approved. Looking back, I could probably have lost my virginity at the party. Conditions were very favourable. She was a nurse *and* English, for example, a planetary alignment then rarely found in Ireland. Unfortunately, or otherwise, Catholicism got the better of me at the crucial moment.

After the party, I didn't see Gary again for a few years. I drifted out of school eventually and into a lowly civil service clerical job – poor Irish ruled out anything more senior. It was my first summer in a Dublin office rather than a hayfield, and I hated it.

Journalism seemed an idle dream at the time. But anything would have been better than where I was, so I applied for various other jobs: equally low paid, just with less of the feeling of a life sentence about them.

It was the early 1980s at this point, though. Work of any kind was scarce and getting scarcer as Ireland descended into deep recession. Sensible civil servants were staying where they were. I stayed too, for a while.

Then one day, I saw an ad for garda recruits and thought: why not? In retrospect, I don't know which of us had a luckier escape, me or the policing profession. We would have been very wrong for each other, I fear.

But those were desperate times for both of us, clearly. So, to my surprise, I made it through the exam and interview and the informal chat with the hometown superintendent who would vouch for you not being a known corner-boy.

Then, in the spring of 1983, I was called for a medical in the Phoenix Park. And who should I meet there but the bould Gary? His father was a garda detective, so maybe this had always been the plan. I suspect otherwise, somehow. My feeling was that Gary had wanted to be something else in life, until fate decided otherwise.

Anyway, we greeted each other like long-lost brothers, comparing notes about football, girls and life in general. I was running a lot at the time and thin as a whippet. Whereas – amusingly for me – the former conqueror of Blayney Faughs now worried that his fitness levels had fallen below what was required for Garda Training College.

It was the last secret he ever confided in me. I was one of a batch selected to see the medics before lunch. Gary was among those asked to come back in the afternoon. So we told each other 'See you in Templemore' and went our separate ways.

I never did see him in Templemore. Soon afterwards, I sat an open civil service exam called the Adult Executive

Officer (so named to distinguish it from the 'Junior Ex', which you could get with a good Leaving Cert). It could have been designed for my special needs, comprising a combination of short English essays and an aptitude test based on ability to process useless information.

My Irish oral was terrible – I was literally sweating with embarrassment during it, listening to the tortured constructions that came out of my mouth – but that clearly didn't matter. I aced the exam and interview and got the job: a promotion to middle management that made civil service life almost glamorous for a while. By the time the guards called me up – many months later – I was no longer available.

Gary had been called earlier, although I didn't know this at the time. Then one dark December evening, I watched the *Six One News* on RTÉ, which led with the sensational freeing in a Leitrim forest of the kidnapped supermarket executive Don Tidey, after a search that had gripped Ireland for weeks.

Two men had died in the shoot-out, however – a garda and a soldier. And as I watched, rapt, I heard the newsreader say that their bodies could not be recovered until morning, because the IRA gang was still presumed to be in the area and the woods were surrounded.

In fact, the kidnappers were already gone. But I remember being struck, first, by the awful heroism of two young men giving their lives for somebody they didn't know, someone deemed by society to be more important than them. Then I thought of their bodies lying in the woods overnight, in mid-winter, and the loneliness – on top of grief – the parents must have felt thinking about their dead boys.

A few minutes later, the phone rang. It was my sister

Pauline, ringing with shocking news. Only then did I learn that Gary had made it to Templemore. He was still midway through the training he had worried about when pressed into the countrywide manhunt and sent to Leitrim. Unfortunately for him, he was the one who found the IRA dugout. Seconds later, he was dead.

I learned afterwards that, by a sad coincidence, our hometown superintendent – who had interviewed me months earlier – was close by him. He was the man who knelt and whispered an act of contrition in Gary's ear.

The next morning, the bodies were taken from the forest by their respective comrades. The army carried Private Patrick Kelly out, while garda officers escorted Gary's remains.

Whenever they replay footage of those events, on *Reeling In the Years* or other TV programmes, I see the guards with the plastic-covered stretcher and know that's him. It still chokes me up every time.

I realise my friend was just one of more than 3,700 people killed during the Troubles. But even though we grew up in a border town, he was the only one of those thousands I knew well.

Every year around mid-December, I wonder what he would be doing now if he were still alive. And, of course, I think about how, but for a twist of fate, it could have been me.

***

Gary earned himself a glamorous funeral at least. TV camera crews descended on Carrickmacross for the occasion. The Garda Band played Dvorak's 'Goin' Home'. Girls from the St Louis convent cried.

'He went out in style,' said one of our classmates, Breifne O'Rourke, as we followed the cortège to the cemetery. And I suppose he did. While most of the rest of us were condemned to grow old, he would now be forever a handsome 23-year-old.

In time, the stand in the local GAA ground was named after him. So, ever since, has been the award for best recruit in Garda Training College in Templemore.

As the major anniversaries of his death came around over the decades afterwards, the Sheehans never talked about him in public. It was still too hard for them. For years, I was in danger of becoming an unofficial spokesman for the family, to fill the gap in reports or documentaries.

This wasn't something I ever felt comfortable about. When you're not used to speaking about such things, you get emotional on camera, which is exposing. On the other hand, you don't want to do it so often that it ceases to move you and becomes a mere performance.

Once, talking about him for a TG4 documentary, I welled up a bit and could sense the cameraman zooming in and holding the shot. Even though tears make for good television, I knew, it felt embarrassing.

Then, sometime later, a producer broke it to me that they couldn't use that interview for some reason. I didn't know whether to be disappointed or relieved. Either way, the next time I was asked to talk about Gary on camera, I said no.

Decisions! Decisions!

For much of my early 20s, I worked in a section of the Department of Social Welfare (DSW) that went by the ungainly title of 'Unemployment Assistance/ Unemployment Benefit Decisions'.

This was usually shortened in correspondence to 'UA/ UB Decisions'. But that wasn't very sexy either. So for several years in the mid-1980s, whenever our phones rang in work, we always picked up the receiver and said: 'Decisions!'

This was a good if cruel joke. Then, as now, I was a natural procrastinator who rarely did anything important today if it could be put off till tomorrow. I need deadlines, preferably urgent, to function, which may be one of the reasons I ended up in journalism.

But in the DSW back then, there was rarely any urgency. Even in a section called 'Decisions', most things could be put off till tomorrow, or next week.

It felt good saying the word, I'll admit. Not even the taoiseach gets to bark 'Decisions!' when answering the phone. If he did, people would think he had notions. Any implication of power in our section title, however, was also a illusion.

As statutorily appointed 'Deciding Officers', ruling on problem cases referred to us by the country's employment exchanges or by social welfare investigators, my colleagues and I were unglorified wielders of rubber stamps.

Some enjoyed the wielding more than others. I had a workmate of slightly Thatcherite bent – he was one of the few men in the office invariably dressed in collar and tie

64

– who affected to suspect that, even at a time when jobs had never been so scarce in Ireland, everyone on the dole was fundamentally workshy.

Whenever you referred a file to him, he had the habit of unsheathing his 'disallowed' stamp – pre-emptively inking it and placing it beside the file – in a manner suggestive of a cowboy loosening his holster flap before a gunfight.

But I think that was just his little joke. Our work was bound by rules, after all, and in a department that dealt mainly with the poor and vulnerable, most people erred on the side of socialism. When disallowing a dole applicant for being 'not available' or 'not genuinely seeking' work, usually we were just acting on a recommendation from the labour exchanges or an investigating officer.

Also, our decisions could always be appealed, and when this happened we were superfluous to further consideration of a case. I was invited to one appeal ever – the appellant could insist on the Deciding Officer attending – but not asked any questions.

For most of the time I spent in the DSW, my speciality – insofar as I had one – was family law. That also sounds grander than it was. Although, to be fair, this was an area where the consequences of a decision could be very important to those on the receiving end. It was also one where, on an almost daily basis, I may have done some good.

The typical case referred to me involved a male, married welfare recipient who was drinking or gambling all his money. This was the tail end of the era when men with families automatically received all the dependants' allowances, even if their wives or partners were on welfare too.

The desperate spouses of such men often pleaded their situation to the employment exchanges, which would then ring Dublin, where a confident-sounding young bureaucrat would answer the phone saying: 'Decisions!' Solomon-like, he would then ask the exchange to secure independent corroboration of the family circumstances from 'a respected third party' – an RTP.

The holy trinity of RTPs then was parish priest, garda sergeant or solicitor. Provided one of those, or someone else of unimpeachable authority, could confirm the family situation in writing, the man in Dublin would advise giving half the welfare recipient's money directly to the wife. It was a discretionary arrangement, and I'm not sure there was any strictly legal basis for it. Either way, in the five years I was making decisions like that, no one ever appealed.

Those cases were easy and could always be dealt with instantly, justifying the billing with which I answered the phone. Then, by contrast, there were the likes of the 'Murphy' file (not its real name), which I could wrestle with for days or weeks without a conclusion. The Murphy file landed on my desk during a period when, briefly, I had been assigned to fraud. Maybe the person who normally covered that beat was on sick leave – I can't remember.

Most fraud cases were routine. By the time the file reached us, guilt would have been admitted and the offenders might already be repaying the money in pittances – 50 pence a week was not unusual – with a promise to increase this if they got a job, which might never happen. There would usually be no need to prosecute.

But the Murphy file was extraordinarily complex, involving as it did a Traveller family. I mention they were Travellers only because their lack of a fixed address – and a multiplicity of non-fixed ones – was central to their alleged activities. Those were multifarious and further complicated by a cross-border element, with simultaneous claims in both the Republic and Northern Ireland. And the case stands out in my memory because it caused all decisiveness to desert me.

The file was at least two inches thick. It covered three or possibly four generations of a family, led by an ingenious patriarch who, according to the investigator, had committed 'every possible permutation' of UA/UB fraud, including claims for fictional children (à la Myles Na gCopaleen's satire of Gaeltacht life, *The Poor Mouth*, although at least the fictional children in this case were human).

The investigation appeared to be a masterpiece too. The trouble was, I couldn't read it. Despite several attempts, I never got much further than the first page. This was because of the investigator's handwriting, which was all but illegible.

The officer concerned was in every other way a model professional. He was so zealous in his work, it was joked that the appearance of his car in the vicinity of a building site resulted in men (those also claiming the dole, that is) scampering down ladders everywhere and fleeing across fields.

And it's not that his handwriting was untidy, like the proverbial doctor's. On the contrary, it was as neat as everything else he did. It's just that his unique calligraphic style did not involve closing any loops, so that his a's and o's looked like u's; his q's looked like y's; and his p's looked like upside-down h's. I spent long periods staring at it, trying to crack the code. But I was as helpless as the early Egyptologists before they found the Rosetta Stone.

The officer acquired a typewriter eventually – or maybe was given one by colleagues, as a hint, or to prevent further suffering. Alas, this was too late to help with the Murphy file.

It must be said that, even in this case, he had succeeded in his main goal: ending the fraud. Once rumbled, the family had fled to England. A successful prosecution or any meaningful recovery of money was now unlikely.

And I can't even remember what exactly was required of me in the case: another rubber stamp of some kind, no doubt, or maybe several stamps. Whatever it was, I failed to supply it during my stint in fraud. The file just sat there on the desk, mocking me every time I picked up the phone and said: 'Decisions'. Just as I had inherited it from my predecessor, I later bequeathed it to whoever came after me.

Ours was not a public office. There was no front counter people could come to, in complaint or inquiry. But occasionally someone would read the small print and present themselves at security, asking to see the faceless civil servant who had ruled on their case.

Once, a nervous female colleague asked if I would go downstairs and talk to an angry man whose payments she had reduced or disqualified. I did and was careful to explain to him that it wasn't me who had shafted him but that the Deciding Officer in his case was indisposed.

And he proved to be perfectly reasonable to deal with, especially when reminded of his right to appeal. Maybe he would have been more aggressive with my female colleague. But he seemed satisfied that a human being had stepped out of the machine and taken time to explain the situation to him.

This was a period when there was talk of making all

civil servants – or the ones who dealt with the public anyway – wear name tags, so that we would not be the faceless stereotypes of old. But there were principled objections, at least in the DSW. Being identifiable to someone whose payments you disqualified could be dangerous, as a colleague was to discover the hard way soon afterwards.

One of the other banes of our life in DSW was the parliamentary question, the PQ. It was a cornerstone of democracy that civil servants should be accountable to members of the Oireachtas. It was also, for the members of the Oireachtas anyway, an easy way to win votes. Some politicians were notorious for their scatter-gun use of the PQ to inquire on the progress of constituents' cases. We cordially hated them for the constant waste of our time.

Once, speaking of politics, I was plucked out of my rubber-stamping routine to make a bigger and potentially political decision. It involved an industrial dispute, of which there were many in 1980s Ireland.

The question was whether we should pay employment benefit to the workers involved. This was usually refused to those who had chosen to go on strike, or even to those who hadn't but who stood to benefit from whatever their colleagues were striking about.

But there were extenuating circumstances in this case. Which one day, much to my surprise, an assistant principal (AP) officer delegated to me. He must also have imposed a deadline for recommendation, or I'd probably still be prevaricating about it now. Instead of which, I wrote a prompt, one-page essay arguing that, while we were legally within our rights to withhold welfare from the strikers, there was both a moral and a pragmatic case for paying them, which was what I recommended.

The AP read it out, not just in my worried presence but in that of another member of senior management. And they both seemed impressed that a mere Deciding Officer could write intelligible English. But after that brief and heady rendezvous with being important, I went back to wallowing in my rubber-stamp obscurity, the charms of which had begun to wear off by about 1987.

I enjoyed my time in social welfare, up to a point. We were on the frontline of a national crisis then. Unemployment broke all records, repeatedly, until almost one in five of Ireland's workforce was on the dole. We had a sense of camaraderie in the trenches.

There were a lot of good people in the department. Smart ones too. A young chap called Martin Fraser joined us during the time I was there, straight from school, in his mid-teens. When I met him again, decades later, he was head of the Department of the Taoiseach and about to become Irish ambassador to the UK.

But I never wanted a career in the civil service and found the job increasingly oppressive. A small yet, to me, intolerable imposition of it was that you were never supposed to leave the office, for any reason bar a fire, during core hours. This was at odds with my desired vocation of sitting in cafés, reading books and newspapers, or watching the world go by. So I slipped out regularly anyway.

I recall having a coffee somewhere once when a man approached and asked if he could borrow my *Irish Times* for a moment. He was on his way to the races in Thurles and had information that a certain horse was going to win. 'Thank God they didn't tip it,' he said, handing me the paper back.

I wondered afterwards whether he meant that it would

have shortened the odds or that the *Times*'s tipsters were so bad he would have dreaded their vote of confidence. Either way, naturally, I stopped into the bookies myself on the way back and had a punt (literally – an Irish £1) on his good thing. Which, sure enough, won, and at odds of 10–1, suggesting that whatever information my informant thought he had, it had not been widely shared.

The important thing is I was a tenner up, and my policy of hanging around cafés had been spectacularly vindicated. This too may have prefigured a career in journalism, a vocation in which being out of the office is (or used to be, anyway) considered a virtue.

Anyway, by the autumn of 1988, I had procrastinated long enough. That October, having put the moment off for five-and-a-half years, I said 'Decisions!' into the phone one last time. Mind you, even this was a fudge. I had merely applied for an unpaid career break of 12 months, which could be extended annually for up to five years.

There being few jobs in Ireland then, my plan was to spend a year working round Australia, and so doing, maybe wean myself off the permanent and pensionable life I loathed. Failing that, I would crawl back and say, well, at least I tried.

The day I left, my principal officer – an affable man with whom I had had few dealings – called me in for a chat. He sounded regretful. 'I don't think we made the most of you here,' he said, as if that was his fault rather than mine. If I ever came back, he added, I was to make sure to come in and talk to him: 'But you won't be back.'

Six months later, I was working night shifts in a zinc smelter in Melbourne when I read the news about a former colleague, a fellow Deciding Officer named Brian Purcell, who had been dragged from his North Dublin home one night and shot in both legs.

It was the brutal culmination of a series of events that began back in February 1988, when RTÉ's *Today Tonight* programme revealed that one of Ireland's most notorious criminals, Martin Cahill – aka 'the General' – was claiming unemployment assistance every week from Dublin's Werburgh Street exchange.

Confronted there by reporter Brendan O'Brien, Cahill covered his face with a hand while pretending innocence of any crime career. Henceforth, in a classic journalistic euphemism, he became 'the man who denies he is the General'.

But in the Dáil the next day, there was consternation and much scorn at the news that Cahill was on the dole and that, while the owner of a handsome private residence in Rathmines, he had also been allocated social housing. Progressive Democrats leader Des O'Malley suggested he must need the two homes for his 'art collection' (Cahill had masterminded the Russborough House robbery of 1986, in which paintings worth £30 million disappeared).

An embarrassed Minister for Social Welfare, Michael Woods, assured the house that Cahill's dole had been suspended. But as some of us knew, that was something beyond the power of even a minister: it required rubber stamping by a statutorily appointed Deciding Officer.

Purcell was the unfortunate officer to whom the task devolved. Later and even more unluckily, he had to attend the appeal hearing – Cahill knew his statutory rights and insisted on them – and sit across the table from the man who still denied he was the General.

For much of the Irish public, Cahill's dealings with the law were a bit of a joke. He played it up himself, turning up for one court appearance in a wig and dark glasses, then stripping down to a Mickey Mouse T-shirt and boxer shorts for the TV cameras outside.

But he was no joke for my colleague. After the dole disqualification was upheld, Purcell received a visit at his home one night from a group of masked men. They tied his pregnant wife up, then bundled him into the back of his own car and drove across the city to Sandymount, near the DART railway line.

There, after a long and terrifying wait, which may have been part of the punishment, they shot him in both thighs. I don't know if it was deliberate on Cahill's part, or good luck on Purcell's, but the bullets avoided bone and artery.

Purcell made a complete recovery in time and went on to enjoy a high-profile career, becoming director of the prison service and later Secretary General in the Department of Justice. But reading about what had happened to him in May 1989, from the safe distance of Australia, I was reminded not for the first time what a mad and dangerous country Ireland was.

Getting out of it, for a while at least, seemed like one of my better decisions.

Generation Game: On the Pain of Rural Migrants Rearing Dublin GAA Stars
14 July 2023

BACK WHEN I WAS A young fella, newly arrived in 1980s Dublin, I briefly had a girlfriend by the name of Bernie Ryan. She was from Tipperary, as Ryans tend to be. And among many other talents, she was a brilliant footballer.

Fast and skilful, she more than held her own in soccer kick-arounds with the lads. But in Gaelic, I think, she played county. Despite her diminutive size, she was fearless in the tackle. I recall visiting her sickbed once as she recovered from a broken collarbone.

Our relationship was a fleeting one. She soon traded me in for a Bruce Springsteen look-alike from Mayo, called Noel, who was also part of our circle then. He was an accountant and clearly a better prospect, because Bernie went on to marry him. But I took rejection well, apart from aiming a few sneaky kicks at him during seven-a-sides in Bushy Park.

Noel had a very exotic surname for a Mayo man: Basquel. Unusual as it was, however, his family were doing their best to propagate it. There were 14 of them, if I remember correctly, including about 10 brothers, all Mayo GAA fanatics.

My theory was that their ancestors had come over with General Humbert in the Year of the French and then missed the boat home, possibly because they were in a pub in Westport, arguing about football. They had since gone native, and not just in Mayo. Last I knew they were also developing a small colony in south Dublin.

Anyway, in our many beer-fuelled conversations of the mid-1980s, Gaelic football was a common obsession. As always, Mayo were on the verge of a breakthrough then. But my own county, Monaghan, was Ulster's coming team.

In the heady summer of 1985, both threatened to break the Kerry–Dublin duopoly that had dominated the previous decade. Our lads won the National League that year, for the first time ever, then added the Ulster title. Barry McGuigan from Clones, meanwhile, became a world boxing champion. So to be a young Monaghan exile in Dublin at the time was to walk with a swagger, even as the dire prospect of meeting the greatest Kerry team of all time in the All-Ireland semi-final loomed.

Mayo faced the Dubs in the other semi and were genuinely confident. One night beforehand in the pub, a member of the Basquel clan explained the pathology of Mayo football vis-à-vis the big two. They never feared Dublin, he said, whereas the mere sight of Kerry jerseys was enough to foredoom them. Amid the ongoing tragedy of Mayo football ever since, that pattern seems to have held true.

In the event, both the 1985 semi-finals ended in draws, before the big powers regathered their forces and won the replays. Secretly relieved that we hadn't been hammered in the first game, despite my outward expressions of utter confidence, I had to compose myself in work the Monday afterwards and affect disappointment.

As colleagues offered congratulations on the shock draw, I shook my head in disgust and said: 'We'll never be that bad again.' In fact, it would be a long time until we were that good again. But in the decades afterwards, there was always a consolation in thinking about Mayo supporters, whose sufferings were invariably greater than ours.

I lost touch with Bernie and the Basquels a few years later. Then life happened, the way it does. Soon another generation somehow rose behind us, taking centre stage.

A few years ago, I noticed a rising new name in Dublin GAA circles: Basquel. There were two promising young brothers: Ryan (what else?) and Colm, both playing under-age for the county and threatening to break through at senior.

Sure enough, eventually, it came to pass. And last week, when Mayo had their hopes crushed yet again, it was one Colm Basquel, son of Noel and Bernie, who did the most damage, with two goals in a Man of the Match performance.

I'm sure parental pride trumps mere county loyalty in such circumstances. If I were Colm's dad, I'd have been cheering for him, primarily. Still, watching from a distance, it was like Mayo's emigration drain in microcosm.

It's a small consolation of advanced age that my own children are unlikely to line out for Dublin, even though that's where they live. Despite – or because of – early exposure to many Monaghan GAA games, they have reached adulthood with no desire to watch football, never mind play it.

In Croke Park this Saturday, alas, I will be alone in my joy or pain. But if the worst happens and the Dubs hammer us, at least I won't have to blame myself afterwards for contributing to their already extravagant reserves of talent.

Go East (and South), Young Man

On the list of the most exciting things that have ever happened to me, just behind the births of my children (and running those close) is the time I won the Japan essay contest. It was 1988 and I'd only entered the competition as writing practice. But as with the children, who happened later, it was a life-changing experience.

Every year back then, young people throughout the European Community (EC) were invited to submit their thoughts on relations between the EC and Japan, in 3,000 words, the best of which would earn a two-week, all-expenses-paid holiday. I had no thoughts on relations between the EC and Japan. I did, however, have a membership of Dublin's ILAC Centre library, where I found other people's thoughts on the subject, of which there were many. I may even have come up with a few of my own in the end.

Either way, one weekend in April, after leaving it to the last minute as usual, I hammered out a 3,000-word summary of my newfound expertise. 'Last minute' is an understatement, in fact. The official deadline had been close of business on the Friday just gone. But I personally delivered the essay into the Japanese embassy's post box at dawn on the Monday, hoping they wouldn't know the difference.

Then I forgot all about it until one dull afternoon a couple of months later, when my phone in the Department of Social Welfare rang. It was the embassy on the other end of the line, with the thrilling news. Suddenly, life was looking up.

Japan was at the very height of its post-war boom then, with a surging balance of payments surplus that had become a big problem for the US in particular. One of the things I recall reading in my library binge was a suggestion by a Japanese economist that his country might consider pegging the dollar to the yen as a favour to the Americans.

What would it expect in return for such generosity, the economist was asked? 'California,' he replied. I'm not sure it was a joke.

The great credit crunch of 1989 was looming, however. Thanks to an asset price bubble and years or over-lending, Japan was about to be plunged into decades of economic stagnation. I don't think that was my fault, exactly. But such was the extravagance of the 1988 essay prize, I do still feel slightly implicated.

A poorly paid civil servant at the time, I had never travelled further than the limits of a European Interrail Pass. It was a dizzying experience to be flown first to Paris, to join 25 other winners from across the continent, and then via Moscow on to Tokyo, business class, with Japan Airlines.

At least I think it was business class. The food, drink and legroom were all liberally supplied. Then again, I may be remembering it through the puritanical prism of decades flying with Ryanair.

But not only were flights, meals and accommodation looked after, our hosts also lavished spending money on us. At an 'orientation' meeting the night of our arrival, we were each handed a brown envelope stuffed with yen: 252,000 of them. Although that probably sounds like more than it is, it was still a lot in 1988: £800 or thereabouts. For me, that was two months' salary, after tax.

Japan was an expensive country, it's true. Left to ourselves, we might have spent the money easily enough. But that's the thing: we were rarely left to ourselves. Most of the trip involved a frantic schedule of arranged events, all free. There was very little opportunity for spending.

Our hosts called it a 'study tour', not a holiday. And sure enough, they were determined to educate us about every aspect of Japanese life. Or at least the aspects that reflected well on the country, which was most of them then.

Our typical day included, say, visiting the Tokyo fish market at dawn, followed by a trip to a Shinto shrine, then lunch somewhere, then a tour of a museum or an architectural showpiece or castle, and after that a banquet.

There was a lot of sake along the way. But sake allowing, among the other bits I remember was spending an evening at a kabuki theatre. We also took part in a tea ceremony. We toured an automated factory near Mount Fuji, watching robots make robots. And we visited a model farm.

There was also a trip on the bullet train – between Osaka and Kyoto. Then they flew us down to the southern island of Kyushu, where we were each allocated to a different family for a weekend, to be given a taste of Japanese home life.

Naturally, the families overwhelmed us with hospitality. In my case, this included a strange but pleasant night in a bar, where the male half of the host couple and I were outnumbered two to one by female attendants – modern-day geishas – who poured drinks, made conversation, laughed charmingly at our jokes and got up every so often to sing.

They didn't just sing: they invited us to sing *with* them. So, standing in front of a strange-looking machine that played music and displayed lyrics, I quietly murdered my part of 'Bridge Over Troubled Waters', and recorded later in my diary that this exotic ritual was something called 'karioki' (*sic*), a phenomenon as yet unheard of in Europe.

There were only two or three evenings of our fortnight left free of scheduled events. On one of these, abandoned by the usual guide, we sought out an authentic Japanese restaurant, off the tourist trail. So authentic was the one we found that nobody there had a word of English. Nor did they have those plastic models of food in the window, ubiquitous elsewhere in Japan, that you could just point at for the waiters.

Consternation ensued. But luckily, one of our number – a guy from Belgian – had studied basic Japanese in Brussels. So for those who didn't like raw fish, he was entrusted to order what he assured everyone were 'steaks'. They were indeed steaks: large, red tuna steaks, as uncooked as the ones we'd seen at the fish market. More consternation ensued.

On another free afternoon, towards the end, I went shopping for souvenirs. It was like being rich, spending thousands of yen on friends and family without a care. Despite which, I still brought more than half the brown envelope money home. Two weeks later, it formed most of the cash reserves I brought with me to Australia, at the start of a 12-month working tour.

Even without the impending credit crunch, that was an epochal time for Japan. Hirohito, the old wartime emperor – once thought of as a god – was nearing his end. After the American occupation in 1945, he had been forced to issue a 'Humanity Declaration', in which he denied his divinity. Now, his frail physique was reduced to a set of vital signs, including pulse rate and blood pressure, reported daily in a fact box on the front page of *The Japan Times*.

Less sombrely, one night near the end of our trip, the group met for drinks in the revolving rooftop bar of a Japanese skyscraper, where a 360-degree panorama of the city gradually revealed itself. In a proud moment, I noticed that their choice of alcohol was strikingly familiar. It wasn't an Irish bar, yet with few exceptions, my fellow Europeans were drinking Guinness, Jameson whiskey or Baileys Irish Cream (a new and fashionable choice at the time).

This was a sign either of Ireland's (or my) bad influence – exporting our national stereotype and infecting others with it. Or it was an early hint of the hitherto unsuspected soft power we yielded abroad as a romanticised underdog, soon to be exploited by the Celtic Tiger. Anyway, it felt somehow encouraging.

The world was our oyster, clearly. This was a comforting thought, considering I'd just spent all my (non-yen) savings on an airline ticket to Perth, a city where I knew no one.

***

The first Christmas I ever spent abroad was in a sweltering Western Australia, at the start of my 12-month working tour. At least it was supposed to be a tour. But since my flight into Perth in October (the cheapest option from Ireland, although a whopping £1,200 back then), it had been all work and no touring.

Perth was a nice place to settle and have a family. If you were 20-something and single, though, it was a bit on the quiet side. I had finally booked a Greyhound bus to Adelaide for St Stephen's Day and looked forward to escaping.

But first I had to break the news to my employer, something that in the run-up to Christmas I had not found a way to do. He was a builder from Armagh, and 'employer' was overstating things from my point of view. I'd been with him only a few weeks and never intended staying longer.

But I needed the money, badly, after a spell as a failed door-to-door vacuum cleaner salesman, which had proved more educational than remunerative. So, although I didn't lie about anything, exactly, I may have been guilty of not correcting the boss's initial presumption that he'd have me for longer than Christmas.

Mentions of the 12-month visa never seemed to register in our conversations. For him, Australia was where you started a new life, nothing less frivolous. Besides, what sane person would think of going back to 1980s Ireland?

Another problem was that we had bonded quickly as fellow Ulster border men, and I suspect he was starting to see me as the son he didn't have. He certainly had longer-term plans. Surveying my weedy frame on one occasion, he said: 'We must get you into a gym after Christmas.' He also mentioned me joining the local GAA club. 'Tell him now!' I heard my conscience screaming. But I didn't tell him.

Building was hard work, especially in an Australian summer, with temperatures in the mid-30s. We had to finish every day by 2pm. That meant starting at 6am, at least for the rest of the crew. During my first week, I was under the impression that the earliest possible train from where I lived could get me to work only by 6.45am, something the boss accepted reluctantly.

Then I discovered there was an earlier, crack-of-dawn

departure. About which – God forgive me – I opted not to enlighten my employer. As it was, at his advice, I had to take salt tablets every morning to avoid dehydration in the unrelenting Perth sunshine. By afternoon, as I slept on the train home, the salt had always reassembled itself into Rorschach test patterns on the outside of my T-shirt.

The other quasi-medical tip he gave me, meanwhile, concerned the dangers of 'going tropical'. A common symptom of this was excessive beer consumption, climate-induced, to which others of his crew had already succumbed. The first time we all went drinking together, I had one beer for every two they had. Even at that pace, I threw up afterwards.

December the 25th arrived and I still hadn't broken the news of my travel plans when the boss invited me to his house for Christmas dinner. This, finally, was where I would have to tell him.

But somehow, again, the moment didn't seem right. I was being treated as part of the family, with his wife and daughter, which only made my imminent defection sound worse, no matter how I rehearsed it mentally.

His wife was more nostalgic about Ireland that he was. She wanted to learn Irish. On her prompting, I recalled some of the words of 'Oíche Chiúin' ('Silent Night'), which she found beautiful, although it also made her homesick.

After dinner we drank beer on the back porch, accompanied by the calming soundtrack of insects hitting the ultraviolet mozzie zapper. A former employee, also Irish, who had since struck out on his own as a contractor dropped in to join us. Back home he had been a member of the Traveller community. Now he was looking for the name of a good accountant, to help manage his expanding finances. He was the Australian Dream personified.

My boss mentioned plans for the New Year again and, for the umpteenth time, I thought: NOW! TELL HIM NOW! But still I couldn't. My resolution fizzled out, like another mosquito on the zapper.

Later, I had to dissuade him from calling me a taxi home. 'I'll get one on the street,' I lied. My budget didn't extend to taxis. Walking the four or five miles instead, in the early hours of St Stephen's Day, I worked on another new plan for confession. This time, it would have to be by phone.

On St Stephen's Day evening, I rang the boss from a callbox, but he was out at the GAA club. So I told his daughter a version of the truth, except that this one involved the sudden offer by someone of a car-share to Melbourne, leaving immediately, which had been too good to refuse.

I also posted him an apologetic Christmas card, embellishing the story. Then I boarded a Greyhound bus to Adelaide. It was a bit like the biblical flight into Egypt, except I was pursued by guilt rather than King Herod on my 36-hour trip across the desert.

***

The most memorable piece of career advice I ever received was given to me in a railway station bar in Wagga Wagga, during the (southern hemisphere) winter of 1989, by a Scotsman with bright orange hair.

Even the hair is hard to forget. It wasn't a shade of orange you would find in nature, among Scotsmen or elsewhere. It arose from misreading directions on a bottle and there was an element of poignancy involved.

Billy – as we'll call him – was a man of advanced middle age, a former British soldier who had become worried about his diminishing employment prospects. Hence his resort to colouring what was left of his follicles.

This shade had been billed as 'auburn', he said. But something went wrong, and the result was a bit more dramatic than planned. He was so embarrassed by it that, when we met, it was covered with a woollen cap, despite the balmy Australian weather and the fact we were indoors.

We were both waiting for trains: in my case up the line to Sydney, in his down to Melbourne. In the meantime, there were a couple of hours to kill with conversation, and I must have been a sympathetic audience.

A beer or two later, when he removed the cap briefly to illustrate the extent of his error, I restrained myself to a rueful smile, even though I was tempted to grab a fire extinguisher and put his head out.

We got to talking about employment prospects because, when you're on a working visa, you're always looking for the next job. I wasn't fussy, having already done stints as a vacuum-cleaner salesman, a builder's labourer and working night shifts in a zinc smelter.

Among the options now, I told Billy, were sheep-shearing and the grape harvest. Which is when he suggested that, if he were my age again, he would forget Australia, go to South Africa instead, and work there as a mercenary, 'assassinating communist agents in the jungle'.

At this sudden turn in the conversation, I found myself studying him again with the same expression used earlier for his hair, while also involuntarily glancing at my watch to see how soon the train was. It occurred to me that, while doing his most recent job – mining, somewhere in the New South Wales outback – Billy might have 'gone troppo', the phrase Australians use for a form of heat-induced madness.

But no, he seemed quite rational, and serious. He was himself a former communist, back in Scotland, he said. Now he hated everything about the Soviet Union and the Eastern Bloc. This overrode any moral quibbles he might have about serving apartheid South Africa, where, he had learned, there was a special corps dedicated to killing the communist agents who were working to overthrow the regime.

The bounty was Aus$1,000 a head, apparently. If you were good, 'you could get three a week'. But Billy was too old for it now. He gazed into his beer sadly, like a man seeing visions of his glory days, when this dream job would still have been feasible for him too. 'I tell all the young army lads I meet that's where they should go,' he said.

Brief as my weekend visit to Wagga Wagga was, I had found that time there passed slowly. The town is world-famous chiefly because of its name, pronounced 'Wogga Wogga', which evokes the romanticised Australia of kangaroos and wombats and the outback in general.

In fact, it's a modern, industrialised place that, being roughly equidistant between Sydney and Melbourne, was once in the running to be national capital, before they built Canberra. Wagga means 'crow' in a local dialect: a dialect that just repeats words to form their plural. Hence 'Wagga Wagga', which can mean anything from two crows upwards; although the sighting of two crows could hardly have been so memorable as to be immortalised in the name. The usual translation implies a place of 'many crows'.

Other things I learned while there is that the town is home to the 'Wagga effect': a phenomenon producing – along with the crows – a disproportionately high number of elite sports performers. This is in turn sometimes explained by another phenomenon, the mythical 'Five O'Clock Wave', said to sweep along the Murrumbidgee River at that time of the evening, so powerfully that it can carry surfers for 100km.

I don't know how real these things are. But not if the Wagga effect had turned me into an Olympic marksman overnight, and the Five O'Clock Wave had then swept me into downtown Johannesburg waving a gun certificate, would I have considered taking Billy's career advice.

Visiting South Africa, even as a tourist, was beyond the moral pale then. As for shooting things, the nearest I had to such experience was as a boy, during duck season once, when a neighbour brought me to help him fetch the felled birds he was expecting. In the event, he didn't hit any.

So I couldn't lie to Billy, even to save his feelings. Romantic as it sounded, I told him that assassinating communists in the jungle was not for me and that the Australian grape harvest was probably a more realistic prospect.

I wonder if any of the 'young army lads' he met were foolhardy enough take up his suggestion that year. For not only was it the most memorable piece of career advice I ever received, it may also have been the worst-timed.

This was only a few months before the Berlin Wall fell, when the map of Europe was about to change colour even more dramatically than Billy's hair. South Africa was on the brink of big changes too. Leaving the morality of his dream job aside, its long-term career prospects would have been very limited.

***

One wet night in Sydney, walking near my youth hostel in a suburb called Glebe, I encountered a pathetically drunk man. He was in a condition that, back home then, we would have called 'paralytic', a word that sounds insensitive now but was more than usually accurate, in this case.

The power in his legs had deserted him, temporarily. He was sitting on the wet footpath and propelling himself slowly along with his hands. So instead of looking the other way, which was my first instinct, I was shamed into intervening, dragging him into a doorway out of the rain and asking if I should ring an ambulance.

Unfortunately, the power of speech had deserted him too. The only word of his I could make out was 'Irish'. Drunk or not, he must have recognised my accent, but I couldn't tell if he was asking a question or offering an autobiographical detail.

Anyway, I left him in the doorway and called the ambulance from a payphone. Then I went back, not five minutes later, to find that the fecker – that was exact word at the time, uttered aloud – had disappeared. The prospect of paramedics, or where they might take him, must have inspired a Lazarus-like recovery, as I had to explain in embarrassment when the ambulance arrived.

I was reminded of this many years later while reading about – of all things – the rediscovery of the HMS *Endurance* in the Antarctic, more than a century after it sank beneath the ice during Ernest Shackleton's ill-fated expedition. Reports mentioned that the ship, now on the sea floor, had been photographed for the first time since the pictures taken by the expedition's own filmmaker, one 'Frank Hurley'.

The Kildare-born Shackleton I knew all about, as I did Tom Crean, another hero of the voyage, from Kerry. But Hurley must have had Irish connections too, I thought, and with that I disappeared down an internet rabbit hole.

As I now know, James Francis 'Frank' Hurley was born in Sydney, on the same Glebe Road I was walking that wet night. His father came from England. And sure enough, the father's father – an earlier James Hurley – was born in Ireland, circa 1821, before getting married in Liverpool in 1849, and then bringing his family to Australia.

He seems to have been a voluntary emigrant, contrary to the stereotype of Irish travel to nineteenth-century Australia. But as it happens, one of the few other recorded details about James Hurley involves a court case from 1856 in Sydney, in which he and his wife were defendants. That too involved drunkenness, although not on their part.

As reported by *The Sydney Morning Herald*, they were prosecuted for theft of clothing and £5 18s from a woman named Ann Jones, after the latter spent a night in their house. The court heard, however, that Mrs Jones had been drunk on arrival, Sunday afternoon, and was at least as drunk when leaving, Monday night.

In between, somebody had undressed her and put her in bed. Then she woke to hear Mrs Hurley saying: 'Begone, for an Irish blackguard, out of my house,' to which Mr Hurley had replied 'You villain, let the woman alone.' After that, she was thrown out 'with nothing but a shift and counterpane on her' and minus the cash, which she had hidden 'in her bosom'.

Confusingly, the 'prosecutrix' also vouched for the Hurleys as friends of long standing and had no complaints against the husband. So the prisoners were acquitted in the end and left court 'without a stain on their characters'.

Their grandson went on to become famous in Australia, not just for the *Endurance* exhibition but also for his pictures from the two world wars. Some of his photographs are considered classics, although he also attracted controversy for using composite images. He defended these as attempts to convey truth more accurately than existing technology allowed. Some critics called them 'fake'.

Speaking of composite images, another thing that often reminds me of that drunk in Sydney is the song 'Tom Traubert's Blues', by Tom Waits. It's about a washed-up sailor, 'soaking wet' and brought to his knees by life and Bushmills. On the plus side, he has a friend called Frank: always a bonus. And even though its subtitle is 'Four Sheets to the Wind in Copenhagen', the song feels Australian, because of its use of the 'Waltzing Matilda' motif.

I doubt my drunk was a sailor, although he could have been. The sea was everywhere in Sydney. For my daily commute there, I had to cross Darling Harbour, get a ferry from Circular Quay and work in a place called Crow's Nest. I also went drinking occasionally in the local equivalent of Temple Bar, The Rocks, where many an ancient mariner must have ended up.

London (and Italia '90) Calling

MAYBE ITALIA '90 REALLY DID inspire the upsurge in Irish economic fortunes that followed it, or maybe that was just coincidence. But for me, the effect set in the week we qualified for the tournament, the previous November, when I won a £25 book token from *The Irish Times*.

It was in the Monday readers' competition, a regular feature of the newspaper then and the inspiration for a lot of bad poetry down the years. The challenge on this occasion was to write an anti-football anthem.

Despite being pro-football, I imagined myself as an employer fearing mass absenteeism on the morning after a big win, so rewrote 'The Auld Triangle', beginning: 'An awful feelin', came o'er me stealin', as I looked at Whelan score another goal ...' It wasn't Seamus Heaney, but it was enough to win the book token.

I was working in London at the time, on a building site, and living in the squat from hell, just off Harlesden High Street. There was no electricity on the ground floor, where my bedroom was: only the lads upstairs had power, borrowed from somewhere else.

So, it being winter, my evenings were spent in the local greasy spoon café, or the pub, or in Willesden library, where a career as freelance journalist in exile took root. Whenever I thought of something that might get into print back in Dublin, I hammered it out on a borrowed portable typewriter and then posted it home.

As for my other home, the squat, that was just a place to sleep. Only when it was time to go to bed every night would I head back to the house, entering via an old sash window that opened from the outside. The others never got around to giving me a key.

Because I also left in darkness every morning, and because the building sites were working flat out in the pre-Christmas rush, I went 14 days once without seeing the room in daylight. Not that I was missing much. It looked better in the dark.

The room had no furniture except a mattress and a settle bed. I usually slept on the mattress, while another guy who didn't have to work and tended to stay out late, or sometimes all night, had the bed.

There was a third occupant of the room, occasionally: a rodent of some kind. We never met in daylight, and I hoped it was a mouse. But one night, louder than usual rustling noises among the crumpled newspapers in the fireplace kept me awake.

Fearing that either the mouse was on steroids, or it was a rat, I promoted myself to the settle bed, which was a slightly more comforting distance off the floor. Luckily, it was one of the nights the bed's usual occupant didn't come home. And I did somehow fall asleep eventually, rodent or no rodent. One good thing about working on the buildings is you were always tired.

Late 1989 was not a good time to be Irish in London, at least not at our end of the economy. IRA bombs were still going off occasionally, and being young, male and from John Bull's Other Island made you automatically suspect.

The deadliest attack that autumn killed 11 army bandsmen in Kent. Where I was working, it sparked a mixture of bravado and fear. 'They were soldiers – they knew the risks,' was the breezy verdict of our sub-contractor, a man from Clare. Then he warned everyone:

'Straight home this evening, lads. This is not a night to get lifted for being drunk and disorderly.'

Back in the parallel universe of football, meanwhile, in December, I watched the live draw for the World Cup, mesmerised by the long, languid fingers of Sophia Loren as she swirled the balls around and, in a historic first, turned a FIFA ceremony into an erotic performance. We drew England again, producing groans of a different kind. Holland again too, a double repeat of Euro '88, with only Egypt to provide novelty for our first World Cup appearance.

Even so, having been in Germany two years before and witnessed the famous defeat of England in Stuttgart, nothing would stop me going to Italia '90. Or so I thought.

The way you looked for work on the London building sites back then was like Ireland's old-style hiring fairs. It was also a bit like new-style prostitution. You just stood on the side of the street in Cricklewood at about 6.30 in the morning, while kerb-crawling builders passed by in vans, eyeing you up. If you looked fit and strong, and your clothes weren't too clean, you got hired for the day at the then going rate of £30, cash in hand.

I only did that two or three times, because if you were any use, you tended to be kept on. Once, however, having taken the overnight train from Holyhead and cycled straight from Euston Station, I arrived at Cricklewood just after 7am. That was too late, it turned out – the vans were all gone already. Secretly relieved, I went for a leisurely breakfast and awarded myself the day off.

Another time I was picked up not by a builder but by a businessman in a suit. En route to our destination, he even gave me his card, which revealed him to be a 'supplier of labour' to industry. In this case, he had a contract with one of the railway companies, which because of health and safety quotas needed a spare man somewhere, for one day only.

Like 'Poor Paddy' in the old song (performed by the Dubliners, Pogues and many others), therefore, I too can claim to have worked on the railroad, albeit only for a single eight-hour shift. Also, 'work' is overstating it. The nearest thing to activity I recall was putting on a hi-vis vest and standing around near the tracks all day, to make up numbers.

It was an easy £30, although the guy in the suit was probably paid a lot more than that for 'supplying' me. Maybe if I'd stayed in London longer, I might have got into the labour supply business myself.

The last time I got picked up at Cricklewood was by a plasterer from Mayo who kept me on for several weeks, up until Christmas. He was a genial man who, like lots of Mayo emigrants, had worked hard and done well in London. He was now building himself a big house in the city somewhere, a fact that sticks in my memory only because I was witness to an event that illegally subsidised the project.

We were helping refurbish a council flats complex at the time, with the various tradesmen doing their thing in order on each block: builders, carpenters, electricians first; then us; then the plumbers. One weekend, under pressure to finish plastering a block before the plumbers arrived on Monday, we had to work all of Saturday and a half-day on Sunday. The plumbers were to install new radiators, which some innocent saw fit to deliver on Saturday morning and leave on site over the weekend. Maybe he thought it would prevent delays.

Unfortunately, one of the rules of London building sites

was that anything not nailed down or chained up got stolen. Despite all the heavy work, there were always light fingers around. If you hung your jacket out of sight, you made sure there was no money in it first. If it was a good jacket, you didn't hang it out of sight.

Leaving unconnected radiators lying around over the weekend was considered criminal in itself. And after we'd finished the plastering job Sunday morning, the Mayo man started packing them all into the back of his van, along with some large sheets of plywood that were also available.

'Are you just ... stealing those?' I asked him, a little shocked at the brazenness of it. He laughed at my innocence. In the morality of the building sites, they were stolen already. It was only a question of whether he took them or left them for someone else later.

Still, the following Monday, everyone knew who'd done it. There were dirty looks from the plumbers but the Mayo man wasn't bothered. They couldn't prove anything, he knew, and would be reluctant to make much noise lest it draw attention to their own stupidity.

One of the last things I did in London that winter – God forgive me – was break a red light while cycling. I won't lie that this was an unusual thing for me to do then. But I remember the occasion vividly because it turned out that the car behind me had a flashing blue light on top, the word 'police' written on the front, and four uniformed officers inside, all of whom then interviewed me at length on the side of the street.

It was my own bike, from home. I had brought it to London on the ferry and train – Ryanair hadn't been invented yet then, so travellers had to supply their own lack of frills. But the police phoned in the serial number anyway, just in case. They also took an intense interest in the novel (no doubt pretentious) in my lunch bag, which in common with the glasses I still wore then, didn't quite fit the story of where I worked.

And although I answered all their questions very, very politely, it was made clear to me that my accent had added to the offence of the traffic light. One of the officers explained that he would be within his rights to bring me back to the station and charge me for something, and that because of 'where you're from', he was tempted. Then they let me go. I didn't break any more lights for quite a while after that.

***

I sometimes envy emigrants, if only for the fact that they get to come home at Christmas. Not that they always do, of course. Even when money allows, pandemics and other events sometimes intervene.

But emigrants have a better chance of coming home than those of us already at home, at least. And for many, it's a magical thing. Only once have I enjoyed that experience in full. It was that winter of 1989 and I had been away for more than a year: first on the 12-month working visa in Australia, then London.

By this point I was a regular entrant in the weekly *Irish Times* readers' competition. I had won it a couple of times, but I was also among the published runners-up on other occasions, something less welcome.

It wasn't just the lack of a prize that bothered me. It was being publicised as a non-winner. I must have felt a need to protect the 'brand', even though I hadn't acquired one yet. So like a pound-shop Brian O'Nolan,

I took to using pseudonyms, and won under a couple of those too.

Anyway, as noted earlier, the competitions often involved writing verse. And it was one November night, while reading the Irish papers in Willesden Library, that I decided the (unrelentingly bad) news from home was worthy of a longer than usual poem.

I wrote this in modified tercet format, with three rhyming lines and a throwaway unrhyming fourth in each verse. The result is all but lost to memory now, perhaps mercifully, and the events it lampooned are forgotten too.

But I do recall one of the more obscure verses, about the president of the Irish Farmers' Association having to resign after a series of controversies, one of which involved him brandishing a shotgun in a dispute with a neighbour.

The verse went: 'Poor Tom Clinton blown away / A shotgun incident ricochet / The army council of the IFA / Claimed responsibility.'

After considering which publication back in Ireland might best appreciate my Swiftian satire on Irish life, I posted it to *The Phoenix* magazine, hoping they might run it in the funny pages of their Christmas annual.

A few weeks later, in classic emigrant style, I caught the train to Holyhead and the boat back to Dublin. Where, putting nostalgia on hold for a moment, the first thing I did was visit a newsagent. I flicked quickly through the *Phoenix* 'Funnies', but there was no sign of the poem. So I said 'feck them anyway' and put the magazine back on the shelf.

Then I returned to my old flat to pick up post. And lo! There among the envelopes was a cheque from the afore-mentioned magazine, for 60 handsome pounds – two days' pay in London.

The cheque was warming my inside pocket when I went back to the newsagents to have another look. This time I bought the magazine. But a more careful trawl of the funny pages again drew a bank.

Then – OMG! – I realised the poem was not confined to the ghetto of the funny pages. It was stripped down the side of Page 3: the inside front. And with a byline – an extreme rarity in *The Phoenix* then or since.

If it hadn't felt like Christmas before that, it did now. At least in my memory, frost suddenly glittered on the footpaths of Dublin. The seasonal lights seemed more delightful than ever. Smiling faces greeted me everywhere. I was home again, among my people. Never had I felt so welcome.

What struck me most about being back in Dublin in 1990 was that, for the first time in my experience, job ads had started to appear in the windows of shops, pubs and cafés. They were 'Mac jobs' mostly, but even so, it seemed like a harbinger of something.

Strictly speaking, I couldn't take up any of these jobs. In return for getting unpaid leave from the civil service, for a year at a time up to a maximum of five, I had to promise not to accept another full-time job in Ireland that somebody else might fill.

Luckily, there hadn't been any jobs when I left in 1988. But by 1990, things were clearly changing. There was enough confidence in the air to persuade me that I too could stay here, freelance full-time and survive. So I did.

On the downside, it had dawned on me by June 1990 that I would not be going to Italy. I watched the tournament Roddy Doyle-style instead, in a blur of Dublin pubs, and chippers, and cavalcades of distressed, pre-scrappage-scheme cars.

Ronnie Whelan didn't score any goals in Italy, as it happened. But under Jack Charlton's game plan, scoring was optional. The morning-after absenteeism happened anyway.

With every game, the rising excitement was tempered for me by the pain of knowing that the bragging rights earned for being in at the start of the mania, in Stuttgart two years earlier, were being overtaken by something greater, something that was going to define a generation.

Oh well. I had a career to launch. So did a lot of other people in Ireland, obviously. A week after the World Cup, the *Irish Times* competition invited readers to suggest something else with which we could now entertain ourselves.

The winning entry – not mine – comprised one word: 'Work'. It was funny because it was true.

A Funny Thing Happened: My Brief Career as a Comedy Scriptwriter

IN THE SUMMER OF AUTUMN of 1990, I answered a mysterious magazine ad seeking comedy scriptwriters for a new, independently produced radio series.

A sample script subsequently earned an invitation to a meeting in an office in the grittier part of Ringsend, where I rang the doorbell on the appointed night, locking my bike to a lamppost outside and wondering if it would still be there when I came out.

Then the door opened, and who should answer it only your man – Dermot Morgan. Morgan was already a star at the time, although his light had been obscured slightly in recent years.

He was still best known for his hilarious contributions to the TV show *The Live Mike* in the early 1980s, when his characters ranged from the unctuous Father Trendy to a frothing GAA bigot who used to attack the audience with a hurley.

But RTÉ had not seemed to know what to do with him since then, and a succession of projects had gone nowhere. Now he was trying again with a series provisionally titled *Scrap Saturday*. The name did not inspire confidence. 'It's a gift to the critics, I know,' he said. 'I can see the headlines: "Scrap this programme!"'

It was a strange meeting. There were only three other people there: a lady novelist whose name now escapes me, a journalist with a Sunday paper (ditto), and a wacky character from Drogheda called Arthur Mathews, not well known then but soon to be half the writing team that would turn Morgan into Father Ted.

It was also one of the more entertaining meetings I have ever attended, because we immediately adjourned to the nearest pub, The Oarsman, where Morgan not only bought the drinks but also gave us what proved to be an exclusive preview of the show.

Charlie Haughey, P.J. Mara, Michael Noonan and Pee Flynn were among the characters who suddenly appeared before us, brought to life by his brilliant mimicry. Morgan was such good fun that, at the end of the night, it felt like a bonus that my bike was still locked to the lamppost.

Having seen the raw material, we were asked to send in scripts, which I did. My working method at the time was to wait until a deadline loomed and then, inspired by panic, write all night.

This ensured concentration, at least. It also had the advantage that you could deliver your side-splitting ma-terial through a post box (this was still the pre-email era) early in the morning, when the intended recipients were still in bed. That way, you did not risk being present when they read it and heartlessly failed to laugh.

So I still remember with horror the morning I cycled down to Ringsend, slipped the envelope under the door (there was no post box), and turned around to a cheerful 'How'r'ya?' It was Morgan, starting work at 7.30am. Before I had time to run, he was ushering me in, sitting me down, tearing open my envelope and reading the contents.

As is a point of pride among comic professionals, he studied the script stony-faced. I was audibly squirming by the time he got to my best bit, at which point he smiled – almost visibly – and said: 'That's a good line!'

Then he laid the pages aside. 'Did you ever think of doing stand-up?' he asked. I knew this was a rejection slip, thinly disguised as career advice. But the only stand-up routine I was interested in at that moment was a prelude to getting out the door, fast, so I didn't seek clarification.

Scrap Saturday duly appeared, 'written by Dermot Morgan and Gerry Stembridge', and the rest is history. It was history all too soon, in fact, because RTÉ took the series off after three seasons, when it was at the height of its popularity.

Political interference was widely suspected, although the show's early demise was in keeping with Morgan's previous relationship with Montrose. 'Every time I work with RTÉ,' he told us in the pub that night, 'I always end up feeling like I've had my bottom felt.'

His horizons were about to widen well beyond Ireland's state broadcaster. But timing is everything for a comedian. And it was a cruel joke of fate when Morgan died suddenly a few years later, as his best years seemed to loom.

He had just finished filming the third season of *Father Ted*, for Channel 4. It's ironic that such a great comic should have become famous as a straight man (or the nearest thing the series had to one).

Or maybe not. Ted Crilly was essentially a mature version of Father Trendy. And Morgan was looking forward to finally leaving the priesthood and doing other things when a heart attack claimed him at the age of 45.

The years immediately before the Celtic Tiger were an interesting time in Ireland. When apologists for Charlie Haughey talk about his legacy, they always mention the free travel, the toothbrushes and the tax break for artists.

They never mention that his last days in power inspired a short-lived flowering of satire.

Yet not only did the era produce *Scrap Saturday*. It also spawned the TV series *Nighthawks* (another target for starving, up-all-night scriptwriters), putting RTÉ executives in the rare position of having two hit comedy shows they could axe prematurely.

I did get a few sketches onto *Nighthawks*, which was quite a thrill. The first was probably the easiest £80 I had ever earned up to that point. One day, after some or other scandal involving Fianna Fáil, I heard someone from the party speak of the need for a 'rebrand', a term commonplace now but new and faddish then.

So I dashed off the script of a 30-second ad, washing-powder style, for 'new, improved Fianna Fail' and, as usual, dropped it by hand out to RTÉ. A day or two later, one of the script editors, Gerry McNamara, called to tell me it was already shot and going out on that night's show.

I felt like hiding behind the sofa when it came on. But McNamara had tightened my words up, added a snappy punchline – 'for a wash so white, you know it's a whitewash' – and generally made it better than the thing I had sent in.

It would never be quite that easy again, although enough of my stuff featured in one form or another in the programme that I later got invited to a couple of scriptwriting workshops in RTÉ. These included the replaying of sketches that had already appeared on the show, which we had to review and critique, an experience I found excruciating.

Most of the others attending were stand-up comedians who wrote and performed their own stuff. And like funny people everywhere, they didn't laugh much: that would be a sign of weakness. So even the best sketches were sat through in silence. The worst, meanwhile, were torn to shreds.

Stand-ups are used to such blood sport: most of them have died a few times on stage while learning their brutal trade. And in their cases, since they performed their own scripts on the show, it was out in the open as to who was criticising whose work.

When one of my scripts came up for review, by contrast, nobody would know who'd written it. I'd have a desperate urge to break the tension and shout 'This is mine!', in hope of either minimising the savagery to come or just embracing the humiliation. Instead, I bit my lip and hoped that my sweating with embarrassment wasn't obvious.

At a season 'wrap' party, I recall chatting with the programme's other script editor, a young woman called Anne Enright. She was a graduate of the University of East Anglia's celebrated creative writing MA and had ambitions to be a novelist. I wonder whatever happened to her afterwards.*

The other memory of that party is that, unlike the Dermot Morgan meeting in Ringsend, it really did cost me a bike. Despite the free bar, I cycled home to my flat safely afterwards but somehow forgot to bring the bicycle inside. I was locked. The bike wasn't. It had vanished by morning.

Scrap Saturday was an overtly political show, whereas the humour on *Nighthawks* was more anarchic. Even so,

---

* This is irony. For anyone who still hasn't heard of her, she did quite well for herself later, winning the 2007 Booker Prize among many other achievements.

it was the latter that led to Haughey's downfall. Not that the sketch writers could claim any of the credit when it happened.

The decisive moment came instead in one of the show's interviews, framed as casual conversations in the *Nighthawks* bar on which the camera accidentally-on-purpose eavesdropped. *Irish Times* columnist John Waters conducted the interview. But the words fatal to Haughey's career were delivered by his controversial former justice minister, Sean Doherty: another funny man whose career-defining performance was in a straight role.

Phoenix Rising: Freelance Journalism in Pre-Celtic Tiger Dublin

BACK IN DUBLIN IN JANUARY 1990, I noticed a strange thing in the windows of some shops and pubs. Suddenly there were signs up saying: 'Staff wanted – enquire within' or variations on that theme.

The great 1980s depression was still casting a long shadow. It would be several more years before anyone coined the term 'Celtic Tiger' – that first appeared in a 1994 investment company report, apparently. But it was clear something was stirring.

I wasn't going to apply for any of these jobs. Even so, it was comforting to know they were there. And it helped stiffen my resolve to stay in Dublin and try to make a living as a freelance journalist.

In the short term, by default, I became more of a comedy sketch writer: not because I thought I was especially hilarious, more because I didn't know any actual journalists in Dublin I could ask about getting work.

Once, I did pluck up the courage to ring Eileen Battersby, who even then was probably Ireland's best-known literary editor (for *The Sunday Tribune*), to enquire if I could review books. Nervously, I made the call from a coin box in Baggot Steet, only metres from the *Tribune* office where she must have been sitting. And it was a surprise when she answered the phone herself. I had expected someone so well-known to have a secretary.

It was an even bigger surprise when, after I blurted out

the reason for the call, Eileen started talking to me as if I was a close friend. For the next 45 minutes or so, she poured out her emotions on a range of subjects, but mostly relating to frustrations with the job. Her literary section had been cut from four pages to two, she told me. There were too many important books that she couldn't fit in. Vincent Browne (the *Tribune* editor) was sometimes difficult to work for. And so on.

I fed coins into the phone and listened sympathetically for as long as she wanted to talk. And after the initial mention, our conversation never returned to the possibility of me reviewing books. But by the end of the call, somehow, it seemed rude to remind her. Even so, I hung up the phone with a feeling of achievement. That was progress, I thought: I'm a confidant of Ireland's leading literary critic now.

Years later, as her colleague in *The Irish Times*, I realised that had been somewhat premature. The truth was, Eileen did this sort of thing all the time. Maybe not with complete strangers, usually. But she and I were never close and yet, on maybe a dozen occasions over the years, in person or over the phone, she opened up to me on the various problems in her life while I nodded in silent sympathy or interjected briefly, like a therapist.

People indulged this and her other idiosyncrasies, with greater or lesser patience, because Eileen was a brilliant literary critic – the best-read person I have ever known. And maybe also because she was a world-class eccentric. Her personality, however challenging, added value to the workplace. Almost everyone had an Eileen story, or a series of Eileen stories, and delighted in telling them.

Another thing I did in 1990 was start writing for the funny pages of *The Phoenix* magazine, which had made my Christmas of 1989 by publishing a comic poem on its inside front page, with a byline, and paid me £60 for it. That was the first and last byline I ever had in *The Phoenix*.

But for the next several years, the magazine kept me alive, while providing a sort of on-the-job training in the basics of journalism. It never paid well. It did pay, however, and promptly, which was more than could be said for many outlets on which freelancers depended then.

For a while, I was writing only satirical skits on the events of the day, which included Italia '90 and the presidential election campaign that featured Brian Lenihan Sr's notorious 'mature reflection' debacle, propelling Mary Robinson into the Aras.

I wrote quarter-page pieces for £25 a time and the more of these they used, the more I gave them, until eventually I was submitting about a dozen per issue, of which they typically printed nine or ten. They were all typed out on paper, old-style, and delivered through the magazine's letterbox. Email was still only a rumour.

I didn't know anyone in *The Phoenix* then, nor they me. But soon I was filling about half their funny pages. So when they introduced a new review section, with 500-word features on various branches of the arts and culture, someone from the office rang to suggest I contribute to that too, as TV critic.

This was the least attractive section, I guessed, involving no freebies. Still, I was happy to do it. Then, a few issues later, they gave me the book review slot as well – a time-consuming job if (unlike Oscar Wilde) you considered it necessary to read the books you were writing about before forming an opinion.

Soon after that, the film critic went AWOL one week, so I took over his job too. And finally, they had a falling out with the magazine's theatre reviewer, whoever that was. I think he breached house style by saying something positive about Hugh Leonard – a man with whom the magazine had a mutually feuding relationship – and then took umbrage when the copy was edited. In any case, I now became drama critic as well.

By this point I was working nearly full-time for the magazine, although it being a fortnightly publication, the workload was lopsided. In the quiet, post-publication week, I would read books, watch TV programmes, go to theatre opening nights, and – a weird new experience for me – attend mid-morning film screenings in empty cinemas.

Then in the earlier part of publication week, I would write up the various reviews. After that, as near as possible to deadline (officially Friday) I started on the funnies, based on whatever was making news. This part typically began on Thursday afternoon and continued all night, fuelled by many cups of coffee, until about 7.30am Friday. Then I would stuff the pages into an envelope, cycle up to Baggot Street, push them through the letterbox and go home bleary-eyed to bed, blinking in the sunlight as I passed commuters on the way to their offices.

All the writing back then happened via a portable type-writer on which, like many old-school journalists, I inflicted unnecessary violence. Or maybe it wasn't unnec-essary. There is – or used to be – an exchange of energy between journalists and their typewriters. Among other benefits, it helped keep me awake at 4 or 5am, when a gentler, touch-typing technique might have been soporific.

In Anthony Cronin's biography of Flann O'Brien, *No Laughing Matter*, he mentions that, while composing his brilliant 'Cruiskeen Lawn' columns, written as Myles na gCopaleen, the real-life Brian O'Nolan used to share a table with his much younger brother, schoolboy Micheál, who would be trying to do his lessons at the opposite end. Such was the racket Myles created on the big Remington, Micheál struggled to work. So eventually they had to put a cloth under the typewriter to absorb some of the noise.

I didn't have to share a table with anyone, luckily. But for a time, I had temporary lodgings in a flat shared by my girlfriend (and future wife) and her sister. And even though there was a sitting room between the kitchen, where I'd be working, and the bedroom where the sisters were trying to sleep, I made enough noise that they too politely suggested a silencing strategy. A folded face-towel under the typewriter did the trick. The sisters of mercy slept better, while I hammered away until morning.

For all this work, at the height of my *Phoenix* career I earned an income that never much exceeded what the dole would have paid for doing nothing. But that was academic, because under the terms of the career break, I couldn't claim social welfare anyway.

In the meantime, I was also receiving a self-administered education in how to keep long stories short. Conversely, in that other prized journalistic skill, I also learned how to write about nothing.

One of the revelations of being a reviewer is how many opinions you have about things, at least when you're forced to go looking for them. I often came out of a film or play, or finished reading a book, whereof I could have summed up my reactions in one word: usually 'meh'.

But then I would have to find another 499 words somewhere. The result was an exercise in mining the thoughts you didn't realise were in you. That was good experience for a daily diary-writing career later.

The other thing I gained from my *Phoenix* sojourn was

a portfolio of sorts, albeit that it was mostly devoid of bylines. The pieces could have been written by anyone. My claims to authorship had to be taken on trust.

In 1992, I learned somewhere that if you were over 27 and had relevant work experience, you could get a place on Dublin City University's MA in Journalism without a primary degree. I now qualified on both these counts, just about.

But I also needed two references and realised, given the anonymity of most of the *Phoenix* stuff, that one of those had better be from the magazine's publisher, John Mulcahy. 'Of course I will,' he said when I asked him to write me one. Then he reached for the phone and added: 'Do you want me to ring DCU and put a word in for you? I know all the people up there.'

This filled me with horror. 'No – don't do that, please,' I said, remembering the dread phrase on civil service job applications: 'Canvassing will disqualify.' I really did fear he would sink my chances by making a call.

'All right,' he said, putting down the phone and frowning as if I was a Jehovah's Witness refusing a life-saving blood transfusion on religious grounds: 'But that's the way things work, you know.'

For a while afterwards, it looked like he was right. First came a letter from DCU saying I hadn't made one of the 25 places on the MA course but was number three on a shortlist, should people drop out. Then there was a second letter confirming that all places had now been taken up. Thank you for your interest, good luck with your career, etc. So much for my hopes of a shortcut MA, I thought.

Around the same time, though, I was also interviewed for a job with *The Sunday Tribune*, which briefly promised work on a national paper without the need for any college education. The advertisement for reporters, remarkably, did not require job experience: music to my ears. But this was a periodic habit of the *Tribune* editor, Vincent Browne, who used it to unearth potential talent from outside the usual gene pool of Irish journalism.

He would then interview all the candidates personally. And here, as elsewhere, he was known for his confrontational style of questioning, which I was now to experience at close quarters.

I didn't get a job out if it, but I did acquire some interesting and permanent mental scars, which I still enjoy displaying all these years later. The main issue of contention was my existing employer. It was common enough knowledge that there was a certain mutual tension – and only a short length of Baggot Street – between Browne and *The Phoenix*. But I didn't realise until the interview quite how much he detested the magazine.

Central to his hostility was the same lack of bylines that bedeviled my portfolio. Journalists were supposed to hold others to account, Browne argued. They could hardly do that if they themselves were unaccountable. Which was a fair enough point.

Unfortunately for me, most of the cuttings enclosed with the job application comprised unbylined pieces: comic skits and reviews. This reminded Browne of everything he hated about *The Phoenix*.

The interview had already gone as badly as I could possibly have feared when – brushing away my latest defence – he reminded me that applicants had been invited to bring what they considered their best piece: 'Have you brought yours?' I wished I hadn't, by then. This wasn't going to end well, clearly. But with all the enthusiasm of a condemned man being asked to oil the hinges of the gallows trapdoor, I handed him a TV review that had been considered a tour de force by Mulcahy and others.

As Browne proceeded to read this opposite me, the interview panel's 'good cop', a man named Michael Hand, filled the tense silence by asking some softball questions about my schooldays in Monaghan. I answered these uneasily, trying to ignore the pantomime of emotions – contempt, despair, sadness – that were playing out on the bad cop's face as he digested my supposed masterwork.

Finally, Hand lapsed into silence, allowing Browne to cut back in. 'Yes, I remember this – you included it with your original application,' he said, correctly. Then he dropped the page as if it had dirtied his fingers and added: 'It's terrible. It's the worst kind of sneering, derisory. . .' Words failed him here. I think he just shuddered instead.

Stung into viciousness, I countered that some people had found the piece reminiscent of the style of Gene Kerrigan. This was a low blow. Kerrigan had been one of Browne's many discoveries – perhaps from an interview like the one I was doing – and until recently a star of *The Tribune*. But, like others before him, he had graduated to better-paid things, specifically *The Sunday Independent*, with its vastly greater circulation and resources.

Mentioning Kerrigan in an interview with *The Sunday Tribune* was like grabbing a broken bottle in a bar room fight. Even so, Browne waved that away too and, pointing at my supposed best piece of journalism, said that if I ever wrote for *The Sunday Tribune*, it would be 'nothing like that'.

I had little to lose by now, so I went on the attack. 'I presume you didn't bring me here just to insult me,' I said. 'Or are we both wasting our time?' Then at last he explained why he'd invited me. It turned out to have nothing to do with *The Phoenix*, or indeed with anything else from my journalism career to date.

Astonishingly, it was my five years as a civil servant in the Department of Social Welfare – an apologetic inclusion on the CV – that intrigued him. He thought this might offer insights into a subject on which his paper was weak and invited me to submit ideas about it for possible news features.

A day or two later, I was further amazed to receive a nice letter from Browne, thanking me for attending the interview and for 'enduring my onslaught against that magazine'. He then went so far as to say I had 'obvious writing talent' – that somehow hadn't come up during the interview – and looked forward to hearing feature proposals.

And I did fully intend to send in a list of ideas. But that same week there was another call from DCU. A place on the MA course had suddenly become available: did I still want it? Yes, I said, but with a sinking heart. Now that I'd had a scent of a real job on a national newspaper, the thought of going back to journalism school was slightly depressing.

Anyway, days later, a decade after the Leaving Cert and aged 27, I was finally a college student. For the next eight months, I attended DCU by day, continued doing my *Phoenix* stuff by night, and earned a 2:1 master's. Alas, then or later, I never got around to writing for *The Sunday Tribune*.

***

A relic of my *Phoenix* days that persisted for long afterwards was Bertie Ahern's secret diary.

The magazine always had a running feature on the

taoiseach of the day, along the lines of *Private Eye*'s 'Dear Bill' (ostensibly written by Margaret Thatcher's husband) or the 'St Albion Parish Newsletter', which portrayed Tony Blair as a happy, clappy vicar.

I had written a spoof John Bruton journal for a while. Then, from 1997, for old time's sake, although I was divesting myself from the magazine by then, I started 'De Diary of a Nortsoide Taoiseach'. It was poorly paid, even by *Phoenix* standards, and in the early years, I tried to dash it off as quickly as possible.

I also tried to give it up on several occasions, but could never quite escape. Someone else would do it for a few issues, then I'd be tempted back for holiday cover, with a slightly improved fee, which in time began to border on the respectable.

When I became the Irishman's Diarist for *The Irish Times* in 2006, daunted by the thought of writing four columns a week, I said: that's it, I'm definitely quitting the Bertie thing now. But even then, it proved impossible. Instead, my *Phoenix* sub-editor Paul Farrell invited me out to lunch one day and said they would double the existing fee if I carried on. It was an offer I couldn't refuse. After that I was stuck with Bertie until his bitter end.

As the title suggests, 'De Diary of a Nortsoide Taoiseach' was written in a sort of phonetic dialogue, but only slightly. Phonetics are weird: people hear and write them in different ways and the result can be distracting to read.

On the other hand, most readers knew what Bertie sounded like anyway. So I opted for a minimalist approach, just enough to suggest the accent, while hamming up his tendency towards spoonerism (upsetting the apple tart, etc.). I half suspect he hammed that up himself.

When his Wikipedia page once described the column

as being 'very mildly satirical', I was almost offended by the 'very'. But it's true that, as lampoons go, it was more affectionate than savage.

Before the tribunals caught up with him and the economy crashed, he was, after all, the most successful taoiseach in living memory. And I still think he was a hero for his part in the Good Friday Agreement, when, among other things, he had to bury his mother in Dublin during a few hours' break from the talks in Belfast.

In any case, the diary's popularity often surprised me. I had the odd experience once, for example, of being in the Leinster House press gallery, writing the 'Dáil Sketch' for *The Irish Times*, and hearing then Labour leader Pat Rabbitte reference my *Phoenix* column as a source of possible insight into the taoiseach. Giving up on attempts to get straight answers out of Ahern, Rabbitte said: 'I look forward to the next "Dairy of a Nortsoide Taoiseach"'.

Circa the year 2000, I also spent a year or two as a full-time political reporter, based in the 'Pol Corrs' room, where 'De Diary' had devoted readers. I recall Emily O'Reilly (then with Today FM, I think, although about to become Ireland's and later the EU's Ombudsman) one day stopping by my desk with the latest *Phoenix* and reading me a bit of Bertie she thought funny.

'That's very good,' I agreed, doing my best to laugh while wondering if she was testing my reactions and trying to out me.

Some people did suspect, clearly. My late colleague Michael O'Regan, who was one of our parliamentary correspondents then, once asked if there was any truth in the rumour I was the secret Bertie.

'No,' I said, 'although you're not the first to suggest it.' I was slightly miffed when he agreed I was an unlikely culprit. 'I think it's John Drennan myself,' he added, referring to a *Sunday Independent* political columnist of satirical bent. 'Yeah,' I said, 'that would be my guess too.'

There were occasions then when, in my *Irish Times* job, I would have to 'doorstep' Bertie (i.e. ask questions of him outside a venue where we had been tipped off he might be) alone, or otherwise meet him in situations where there were no other journalists present. Obviously, those could never feature in his secret diary, however tempting it sometimes was.

I don't know if he ever read the column himself. But there was an odd turn of events in 2008 when his run as taoiseach, and by extension the *Phoenix* column, both ended. The magazine decided to publish a book-length anthology of the 11-year-series and asked – who else? – Bertie if he would launch it.

In a case of life imitating art ('art' may be pitching it a bit high, I know), he agreed. Then something else came up and he couldn't do it. In the end, Conor Lenihan deputised. Among other things, the event was my own first book launch, although I thought better of attending it myself.

The Night I Had John Hume
in My Car
30 October 1999

MY NOISY OLD CAR AND the Northern peace process have
a lot in common. They've both lasted more than a decade
now, for one thing, but it's only in recent years that either
of them attracted serious public attention.

They've both had major setbacks, too. And the pace at
which they move has become frustratingly slow, especially
over the past year.

Even so, until now, neither one had irretrievably broken
down. Whereas, at time of writing, each is undergoing an
official review process, one in Stormont and the other in
a garage in Monaghan.

The other thing my car and the peace process have in
common is that John Hume has featured in both. But we'll
come back to that in a moment.

I bought the car from the proverbial one careful female
owner and, by and large, it has served me well. It does,
however, have a history of letting me down at crucial
moments, most notably the night my daughter was born.

It chose to mark that impending occasion by breaking
the front section of its exhaust. We announced the birth, not
in the social columns, but by roaring across the city to Holles
Street at 4am, rousing frightened pigeons from their sleep.

My wife may have been in labour, but she still wanted
to get out half a mile from the hospital and walk the rest
of the way. I had to tell her this was no time to be feeling
embarrassed, and drove right to the door.

In recent months the vehicle has been accumulating

problems. Someone hit the side of it in a car park and didn't let on. It was too expensive to fix, since I planned to trade it in soon, so I didn't.

Then the back section of the exhaust went, and the garage didn't have the right part at the time. But because the problem was only a rattling noise, I wasn't sufficiently moved to go back to the garage since.

More worryingly, the engine had been labouring in the lower gears of late and was going up hills like an articulated lorry with a puncture. Even so, it continued to perform well enough on the flat, so I wasn't unduly worried when asked to drive to Donegal last week to interview John Hume.

And we were still in good shape as I drove down the steep lane to his seaside house, fretting only that the car might struggle to get back up. For the moment, that was secondary to my fear that Hume would see the thing I was driving, so I parked a discreet distance from his front gate.

Shortly into our interview, alas, the SDLP leader suggested we adjourn to a restaurant in the local village and, immediately, alarm bells went off in my brain. I made a mental calculation that, having just undergone stomach surgery, my interviewee probably wasn't able to drive, while walking was out of the question too.

Then I heard myself ask if we should take my car, while offering a secret prayer to the patron saint of embarrassment that the answer would be 'no'. The prayer didn't work. In Northern Irish politics, 'no' is what Ian Paisley says. John Hume, of course, said yes.

It's not every day you have a Nobel Peace Prize winner and living legend in the passenger seat of your car, and when it happens, it would be nice if it was a new car. Or, failing that, a well-kept second-hand one.

But it's from situations like this that you learn the art of poise. It isn't easy when your door has a big dent in it, and the exhaust is rattling, and you can only make it up a hill in first gear and – Oh God! – you've only now noticed the week-old milk stain on the passenger seat where the baby threw her bottle, to turn casually to your passenger and ask: 'So, how do you think the Mitchell Review is going?'

Yet somehow, I did. And apart from a feeling of mortification that will follow me to the grave, the incident passed off well. We made it safely to the village, did the interview, and then made it safely back.

I should have known, though, when John Hume said in parting, 'You need to get that car looked at soon, or it'll leave you in the lurch somewhere,' that his words would prove, as so often in the past, prophetic.

Me and the car had harsh words afterwards, as we drove home through Derry, and that may have been the final straw in our relationship. We had just reached Newtownstewart when the vehicle started slowing down for no apparent reason. And we were in the middle of the town's main street when it ground to a complete halt.

I didn't know then, but the clutch had gone. I only knew that, in peace process terms, the car was refusing to move the situation forward, or indeed backward. And that, since it was late Saturday night, the chances of my finding a mechanic locally were about the same as me being served alcohol at the next DUP conference. I had no choice, given the car's intransigence, but to stage a walkout.

Newtownstewart is a Protestant town, and I knew my predominantly Catholic vehicle would attract suspicion if I just abandoned it. Indeed, as I locked the doors, I told it – cruelly – that there would be a British army robot along shortly to attach an explosive device to the boot (it's terrible when your relationship with a car turns bitter).

But to forestall just such an occurrence, I went to the local police station to inform them my Nissan Sunny would be staying in town for a while, or at least overnight. Luckily, my sister Pauline lives near the border, and she was able to come and collect me at no greater inconvenience than losing half the night's sleep she had planned before going to work very early next morning.

Even more luckily, her brother-in-law happens to be a mechanic with a pick-up truck, and he was able to liberate the vehicle in a daring pre-dawn raid. Now the same man is attempting, Senator Mitchell-like, to put together a deal that will allow me and the car to live in peace. And for my part, I'm prepared to work the process, and to put the bitterness of the past behind us and move forward again together.

At least until I get an answer to this small ad:

1989 Nissan Sunny for sale. Two prev. owners, one careful. Small dent in door, otherwise mint cond. Many extras, incl. new clutch. Once sat in by Nobel P.P. winner, Any reas. offer cons'd.

Three Weddings, a Funeral and a Job: The Long, Hot Summer of 1995

THE 'WEATHER STORY' IS A staple of print journalism, especially on quiet news days. And when you're a lowly freelancer, you get to write it a lot.

So I can say with some authority that the summer of 1995 was the hottest in Ireland since records began. June, July and August averaged two degrees Celsius above normal, almost everywhere. August was exceptionally warm and dry, with a high of 31 degrees recorded in Kilkenny on the second.

The American humourist Dave Barry, a hero of mine, visited the land of his ancestors that year. When I met him at home in tropical Miami a few years later, he was still scarred – or pretending to be, anyway – by the ferocity of the Irish summer.

They're used to heat in Florida. But Dave and his wife came here expecting rain and mist and packed accordingly. Instead, they found themselves unable to sleep because the hotels didn't have air-conditioning.

'We scoured the hardware stores looking for a fan,' he told me. 'But the fans were all sold out.'

It was hot even in late April, when my father died. There was nothing sudden about his death. The decline had started two years before, when, one day after Christmas, he suffered a mild heart attack.

I remember him putting on his suit to go to hospital, the way older people do, with the look of a man who wasn't sure he'd be coming home again. But he did get home, eventually. And in his last two years, I made a point of trying to converse with him more often, penetrating the pipe smoke and silence that generally surrounded him. It was a mixed success.

By the spring of 1995, he was back in Louth County Hospital, this time to stay, and mostly beyond talking. We all took turns to spend nights with him. Twice a week I'd get the train up to Dundalk, armed with a book and a baby Jameson to shorten long hospital nights in a chair. In the mornings, I'd walk back along the Carrick Road, past the Harp Brewery, to the station, feeling relieved and guilty to be out in the barley-scented fresh air again.

A moving thing happened near the end. By coincidence, our long-estranged neighbour ('Pipes' as we called him, although his real name was Pete) was also in hospital, two wards away. He and my father had been good friends in their younger days, but they hadn't spoken to each other for 33 years – except once in a row caused by a 10-year-old me – because of one of those classic Irish grudges about land.

My parents always insisted Pete was a good man who had been led astray by a certain other party, now long dead. Even so, the silence continued until late April 1995, when a delicate peace process brokered by my mother unfolded.

One day, at her prompting, Pete walked into my father's ward, shook his hand, and said he'd pray for him. It was a short conversation after 33 years, but it was enough. He had made his peace with my father while he still could. He would be dead too by autumn.

In an echo of a certain romantic comedy of the previous year, our family had three weddings scheduled for the summer of 1995, including mine, and a fourth in 1996. In our case, the funeral came first. There had been several false alarms by then, for each of which we all gathered, only for my father to rally again.

When the final moment did come, I missed it. I'd been stuck in the middle of a boring news feature for days and was trying to finish it before leaving Dublin. Then, when it became clear that this really was the end, my brother was dispatched from the hospital to bring me home, and he missed it too. Still, my mother and five sisters were all there when it mattered, so my father was blessed among women till the end.

There wasn't much time for mourning, meanwhile. With my younger sister Patricia getting married in July, I was now suddenly the family patriarch and would have to 'give her away', in that quaint phrase. I was due to give myself away in early September, then another sister, Pauline, the same month. It was a summer clearance sale in the McNally family: almost everyone had to go.

Work had become uncertain. The term 'Celtic Tiger' was by now in use and the boom was starting to be felt in most places. But freelance journalists were at the bottom end of a trickle-down economy. Casual shifts in the *Irish Times* newsroom were scarce. Jobs were only a rumour.

Worse still, *The Irish Press* group was now on its last legs, and we all dreaded the expected flood of asylum-seekers soon to be washed our way from Burgh Quay. It seemed like a bad year to be getting married.

Most of my shifts were what is known in the trade as 'Night-town'. This is the graveyard beat, which then ran from 9.30pm to 3.30am. It had a reputation for driving journalists insane.

After midnight, you'd be propping up your eyelids in between ring-arounds of provincial garda stations, where night sergeants would invariably inform you that, no, there was nothing stirring. Anyone worried about crime levels in Ireland should try ringing provincial garda stations at night to ask if anything's happening. It's very reassuring as long as you're not in the news business.

I don't know if it was the weather, or delayed mourning, or what, but sometime in June a wave of gloom overwhelmed me. Paradoxically, the endless sunshine seemed to be part of it, at least. For weeks I would wake up at dawn with a knot in my stomach thinking, like that woman in the film *White Mischief*: 'Oh God, not another fucking beautiful day!'

Some of it was work too. Except for the weather story, everything I wrote about that summer seemed to be on the theme of mortality, from heat-related fish kills to a grisly triple murder case in Cork.

I spent a week on the latter story, traipsing around Mayfield on the city's northern edge, where gardaí were digging for bodies. One day I made the mistake of walking up a lane near the scene marked 'private', where I was met by a hostile farmer who clearly didn't like trespassers but, just as clearly, was enjoying the area's notoriety.

Ordering me off his property, he quipped: 'I've enough land here to bury you in.' I turned my back on him nervously. The walk back down the lane seemed a lot longer than the walk up.

There's no good time to be depressed. But it's particularly bad timing when you're a freelance journalist trying to appear enthusiastic, and when you're also about to get married.

Luckily, being male, I was mostly superfluous to the organisation of the wedding, in which my main role was to turn up on the day and stand where I was told. That and arrange the honeymoon. So, while Teresa busied herself with the logistics, I took a few days off work in early August and went to Lourdes.

Actually, Lourdes was incidental to the plan. Before Ryanair, empty seats on Aer Lingus pilgrim charters were a cheap way to get to the south of France, where I hoped that a few days in the company of Bertrand Russell's *History of Western Philosophy* would dig me out of whatever hole I was in. I could then maybe subsidise the trip with a travel feature on the pilgrimage business. It wasn't much of a plan, but it was something.

Despite hosting many of the tackiest souvenir shops on earth, Lourdes – where my parents had been several times – is not without its charms. I steered well clear of the baths, sticking to the cafés and immersing myself in French beer instead.

But I think I was also half hoping for a spiritual cure of what ailed me. By passively inhaling the faith of the thousands of believers, maybe I would regain the sense of purpose that seemed to have deserted me.

I didn't understand what was happening, really. Although I liked my father, I had never been close to him. And his death was so well foreshadowed, I can't say I was stricken with grief afterwards. But no matter how little a surprise the event is, I suppose, it's still a deep shock to realise that a person you've spent your life wanting to impress is gone forever.

Anyway, sometime around the start of September, the weather broke at last and, with that, my gloom mysteriously lifted. Two days before the wedding, Hurricane Iris (although downgraded to a severe storm) swept Ireland, bringing heavy rain to most parts. The effect must have been electrifying because, a full 24 hours in advance, I finally got around to organising the honeymoon, or at least a flight to Rome.

The trip started badly when I inadvertently booked us into the world's worst hotel, near Termini railway station. Apart from general awfulness, the only thing I can remember now is that the bathroom door was fully detached, just leaning against the wall to cover the gap.

But then we headed south to Naples and Sorrento and things picked up. We spent an afternoon in the ruins of Pompeii, mesmerised by the setting, the smell of pine trees, and the knowledge that we were walking on 2,000-year-old streets where all life stopped on a known day in the year AD 79.

From there we took a boat to the Isle of Capri. As we crossed the straits at dusk, a lightning storm lit up Mount Vesuvius behind us, adding drama to the romance. I hadn't planned the special effects but claimed the credit anyway.

***

Somewhere in the middle of all this, a job came up in *The Irish Times*, for Crime Correspondent. I had no ambitions to be a crime correspondent, and as often happened at the newspaper, there was somebody already filling the role, informally. Everyone assumed (and we were right to) that he was a shoo-in for the official position.

Even so, all the regular freelances applied, as they were expected to, by way of demonstrating ambition. I followed suit but then blithely failed to prepare for the interview, because what was the point? When the day came, I breezed in and out of the room with nonchalance and then congratulated myself on how well it had gone, all things considered.

This must be what psychologists call the Dunning-Kruger effect: the sublime confidence of those who don't know enough about a subject to realise how little they *do* know. Afterwards, two different editors who had been on the interview panel took me aside to explain that, in fact, it had not gone well for me at all. Among other things, for example, I had been unable to answer a question about how many known heroin addicts there were in Ireland: basic information for any crime reporter.

OK, I probably wasn't going to get the job regardless, they both admitted. But there would be other jobs down the line, for which they might be trying to argue my case to sceptical superiors who didn't know me as well as they did. With my half-arsed crime interview that day, I had not done them any favours. Chastened, I apologised to both and promised not to make the same mistake again, if the chance arose.

Then in early 1996, sure enough, *The Irish Times* advertised for three general reporters. They were the first such new jobs at the paper for nearly a decade, and among the many people who applied, there seemed to be a long list of candidates better qualified than me. Those included veteran reporters from *The Irish Press* group, which had folded the summer before.

So again, I didn't expect to get one of these positions. But I was on notice this time that, if invited to interview, I needed to perform. And whatever the opposite of the Dunning-Kruger effect is, that set in now. No amount of preparation seemed enough.

On the night before my 10am interview, I couldn't sleep. Next morning, I threw up from nerves, something that has never happened before or since. Assuring myself I had no chance of getting one of the jobs – so there was nothing riding on this really – didn't help. It still felt like my life was on the line. I might as well have been walking to the gallows.

Apologies in advance for claiming to have anything in common with the great Irish football player Liam Brady. But the story goes that, before his international debut against the Soviet Union in 1973, he was so nervous in the dressing room that a more seasoned teammate quietly told player-manager Johnny Giles not to play him: 'His bottle's gone.'

Giles picked him anyway, then made a point of passing the ball to Brady straight from the kick-off, and the debutante went on to deliver a midfield masterclass in a famous 3–0 Irish win.

So, sometimes at least, nerves can be your friend. Twenty minutes before the interview that morning, still sick with fear, I was tempted to just not turn up. Then at about 9.50am, miraculously, all the nervousness vanished.

From there on, my confidence was bullet-proof, and this time I had the right answers to go with it. When it got to the bit at the end of the interview where they ask if you have anything to add, I did indeed have something to add. I can't remember what it was now, but pressing home some point or other, I felt like – renewed apologies for the football analogy – Don Givens completing his Brady-assisted hat trick against the USSR.

A few days later, when they announced the successful candidates, it should have been a triumph. In fact, it turned out to be an uncomfortable experience. My fellow chosen ones, Alison O'Connor and Catherine Cleary, had the good luck to be off that day, or working elsewhere. But I was on a morning shift in the newsroom, where there was blood on the carpet.

I watched sheepishly as a freelance colleague who had been widely expected to get one of the jobs returned in tears from Bewley's Café, where an editor had explained why she hadn't. Later, a senior staff member arrived in work and, after quizzing me for news of the announcements, forgot the bit where he was supposed to say 'Congratulations, Frank'.

Instead, he lamented the fate of someone else he had hoped would be picked. 'He's fucked now,' he said. The person in question was far from fucked: he too would be staffed soon afterwards and go on to enjoy a highly successful career.

In fact, many of those who didn't succeed on that occasion would get jobs eventually. With the economy increasingly rampant, the newspaper's most commercially successful decade lay ahead. But the great 1980s recession still cast a long shadow and, even in 1996, those reporter appointments had seemed like a make or break for many.

Alison was at home in Cork that day. When she rang to share her excitement at the news, I had to keep my voice down out of respect for the temporarily vanquished.

It was a life-changing moment, even so. Eight years on from quitting my permanent and pensionable civil service job, the gamble had paid off. And after an especially turbulent 12 months, I went home to my new wife that night a staff reporter on *The Irish Times*.

Waist Management:
On Dealing with a Midriff Crisis
12 December 1998

THERE COMES A TIME IN every man's life when he needs to take a long, hard look in the mirror and ask himself the question: where did that belly come from?

I was hoping to have to deal with this around the same time as another question: a yacht or a holiday home in Spain? – what *will* I do with all this money the company gave me for my early retirement? But that was before I turned into a metaphor for the Irish economy.

I first noticed this trend last year, when experiencing a record 7.5 per cent growth rate. Following another buoyant set of returns recently, however, it looks like the growth rate could reach a staggering 9 per cent for 1998;* and when you include the 5.5 per cent achieved in 1996, this amounts to a period of sustained expansion matched only by the Irish economy's.

The inflationary tendency has been most noticeable in the key economic indicator of 'shirt size'. As any economist can tell you, figures can be massaged by a well-cut suit, but shirt size doesn't lie. Under this heading, I broke through the psychological 16-inch barrier in mid-1997; and according to the latest figures, I'm about four pints of Guinness away from breaking the even more psychological 17-inch barrier.

When they talk about the Irish economy 'overheating', I know exactly what they mean. When I walk to work

---

* Figures for December not yet in.

now, I have to loosen my tie after the first half mile, even in sub-zero temperatures.

And the worst thing is that all indicators suggest this growth could continue well into the next century, with equilibrium setting in only when I reach the size of Helmut Kohl (whose own expansion started when he became a metaphor for the German economy in 1951).

There are some obvious causes of this weight gain, the nature of my job being the most obvious. In journalism, for technical reasons a layperson could not be expected to understand, lunch can last for up to four hours and is often followed immediately by dinner. It's no coincidence that the last year I experienced negative growth was 1995, when I was a 'freelance' (which is to say, a person who can't afford regular meals).

Clearly, drastic economic measures are called for. But the problem, familiar to finance ministers everywhere, is how to slash spending on food and beer without precipitating a state of deflationary depression?

The only other option is increased exercise, but what kind? Ten years ago, when the economy and I were both very underdeveloped, I would go for a run regularly (like the Irish pound) and had about as much body fat as the state had budget surpluses.

But then you get to a certain age when the idea of having working knees past the age of 40 becomes important, so that was the end of the running, for a while.

Cycling seems a good bet – I used to do a lot of that too. But go for a cycle in Dublin traffic these days and you soon find yourself thinking about safer forms of exercise, such as climbing ESB pylons.

Which leaves only football. And as regular readers will know, I'm already a regular football player (of the type known in the sport as 'crap'). The problem with football is that the older you get, the less actual physical exercise you derive from a game.

Against which, when younger players skip past you as though you're not there, you may lose weight from embarrassment. Even here, though, there are diminishing returns. A sense of shame is one of the first casualties of playing football into your mid-30s, and after a while, you can let younger players beat you without a thought.

And now I've learned that one of my co-footballers broke several bones in his foot in a harmless-looking fall on AstroTurf recently. His doctor showed no sympathy, telling him he sees the same thing every week with players who are too old and unsupple to play on a surface which (like the doctor) is notoriously unforgiving. I wouldn't be so worried about this except that the guy in question was one of those who used to skip past me as if I wasn't there.

One thing I've never tried is fencing, for which suggestion I have to thank a concerned reader, Shirley Duffy. Shirley runs a fencing school and on foot of a recent column in which I suggested we bring back duelling to ease pressure on the courts, she wrote to me agreeing, but suggesting swords rather than pistols.

She also pointed out – and I think this risks taking the fun out of it – that there are excellent rules nowadays for avoiding fatalities (I don't like to say it, but this sounds like naked self-interest on Shirley's part: no business likes to lose customers).

Nevertheless, sword-fighting does look like a fail-safe idea. As a swordsman, you have two options: (1) move very fast on your feet, or (2) have lumps cut out of you. Either way you lose weight. On the other hand, the same seal-like mobility which has dogged my football career would probably be a big drawback in fencing too.

But I need to do something. A drastic cut in calorie intake or a new form of vigorous exercise that doesn't endanger any vital body parts? It's a tough choice: I'll have to think about it over a pint.

Be Careful What You Wish For

ONE OF THE REASONS FOLK wisdom warns us to 'be careful what you wish for' is that, by the time you get whatever it is, often you're no longer the same person who first wanted it. My appointment as the *Irish Times* Diarist in 2006 is a case in point.

When the news broke, a friend from my journalism MA class of 13 years earlier texted congratulations: 'It's the job you always wanted!' But I was puzzled that she thought so. If it had ever been true, or even if I'd said it one night in a pub somewhere, the memory had evaporated.

The truth in May 2006 was that I didn't want it, really. When the long-time incumbent Kevin Myers suddenly stopped writing the column a month beforehand, after one too many rows with *Irish Times* management, it never occurred to me that I might become his replacement.

On the contrary, any time the subject came up in conversation, as it did regularly during the hiatus when his return was still a possibility, I was heard to suggest that if he didn't come back, the paper should just retire the column with him: 'It's a poisoned chalice for anyone else now.'

The 'Irishman's Diary' (as it was still called then most days, although it was also often 'An Irishwoman's Diary') had traditionally been a quirky, humorous, slice-of-life feature. So it had remained for much of Kevin's reign too.

But Myers also had a great talent for polemic and, as the years passed, his 'Diary' seemed to become more and more fiercely opiniated. This generated countless Letters to the Editor, with which he shared a page in the print edition: half of them from outraged feminists, republicans and other regular targets of his typewriter, the other half welcoming evidence that at least one columnist in the paper had sense.

Kevin seemed to revel in the notoriety, most of the time. And much of his output was undoubtedly brave in standing against the consensus of the day. But sometimes, at least, he seemed to be punching down, against targets less powerful than himself. More generally, I think, he also became a prisoner of the need to be outrageous. It cost him in the end.

About a year before his final break with the newspaper, he wrote a now notorious column about single mothers and the social welfare system. At its centre was a point worth making: that because motherhood conferred housing and other benefits on young single women with few other advantages in life, the state was creating and perpetuating poverty traps. Alas, that message was overshadowed by his decision to call the women in question 'mothers of bastards' (shortened in subsequent mentions to 'MOBs').

The ensuing furore blew up far beyond the *Irish Times* letters page, which would have vented – and did – the usual rage at a columnist whose style, however annoying to some, was at least familiar. That would have played itself out, safely, within the *Times*-reading community. Instead, the MOBs column also quickly became the stuff of radio talk shows and of tabloid newspapers whose audiences had never heard of Kevin Myers.

There was initial reluctance by the Editor's Office to let him go on air and explain himself or apologise, lest he only make things worse. By the time he did so, it was too late.

And yet that wasn't the final straw for Myers as Diarist. The end came a year afterwards, when the paper published a 16-page supplement to mark the 90th anniversary of the 1916 Rising. This was a superb piece of work, comprising mostly original reportage from the period, which many of us were reading for the first time, although it would become much more familiar during the centenary commemorations a decade later.

And it was a deliberate decision that there would be a minimum of editorial comment in it, apart from one 'think-piece' by Fintan O'Toole. Or so the editor Geraldine Kennedy told me on the day she asked me to be the new Diarist.

But the old Diarist, for whom 1916 (of which he was an ardent critic) had long been a running theme, took his exclusion from the supplement as a snub. He never wrote for the paper again.

I didn't know this at the time. All I knew is that from then on, for a month or so, the 'Diary' was written by stand-ins, something that happened two days a week anyway and whenever the Chief Diarist was on holiday.

At first, I thought Kevin was away or off sick. Then the Sunday papers reported that he was in negotiations about a move to *The Irish Independent*. After that, I assumed he was just taking advantage of a random job offer, perhaps to improve his position in the existing one, as any rational person would.

It never occurred to me to ask anyone in the Editor's Office what was really happening. The word down in the newsroom, meanwhile, was that it was a sensitive issue but that contacts were continuing and the paper had not given up on his possible return.

In the meantime, in what I didn't realise was one of my final 'Last Straw' columns for the weekend edition, I made an innocent joke about the 1916 supplement, which was to have unfortunate consequences for my friendship with Kevin. The joke involved a historic parallel: discussing the supplement as people had once discussed the Rising itself.

It ran as follows:

Posterity will decide whether this newspaper's 16-page supplement to mark the 90th anniversary of the Easter Rising was justified. Some may argue that the stated aims of the signatories ('to return, insofar as possible, to the lived reality of the Rising', as Fintan O'Toole wrote) could have been achieved by less drastic means. No one, however, can doubt the bravery and idealism of those who took part.

I was among the gradualists who believed we should hold off for the 100th anniversary before going big. No doubt that's why I wasn't invited to get involved, although I knew for months that something like this was planned. As Yeats said, I have met them at close of day, coming with vivid faces from counter or desk among grey eighteenth-century houses (we're moving to a new building in Tara Street soon, and not before time). Anyone could see they were up to something.

Despite the frivolous nature of this riff, it drew a very serious response from one occasional correspondent, who wrote to me criticising the supplement for its lack of a retrospective opinion piece making the case against the Rising.

I should just have ignored this. But I replied, pointing out that the omission lamented by the emailer was the sort of thing Myers might have written had he been involved and guessing that he had been excluded because of his 'apparently imminent defection' to *The Independent*.

As I soon found out, this was me putting cart before horse. And the way I found out is that the person who had written to me happened to be a friend of Kevin's and forwarded my reply to him. This in turn provoked Kevin to send an angry email – the only one I recall ever receiving from him – setting the record straight while accusing me of adding to an *Irish Times* campaign of misinformation and other forms of disloyalty.

Now it was my turn to be hurt. I had always liked Kevin. In my early days in *The Irish Times*, we shared a corner of the newsroom. And having read him since my teenage years, I was somewhat in awe. But I also found him good company.

He was educational, encouraging, sometimes even protective. Once, as a newbie freelance, low in self-assurance, I was audibly stunned by the hostility of someone (an Australian executive with a Dublin radio station that had suffered bad figures in the latest listenership survey) I called for comment.

'Who was that?' Myers asked after I'd put the phone down, feeling embarrassed and humiliated at a loss of confidence that had been public for anyone in earshot. Before I knew it, Kevin picked up his phone and rang the man, intent on subjecting him to some of the same medicine. Luckily for all three of us, he didn't get through.

I also used to marvel at the state of Kevin's desk: an ergonomic disaster comprising a mountain of paper – readers' letters, cuttings, books and magazines – on the foothills of which, placed at a slope, was his keyboard. But that was instructive too. It was a filing system of sorts, one I gradually came to adopt myself, for good or bad (although I have always made space to keep my keyboard horizontal at least).

He used to call me a 'Border Fenian' – an affectionate (I think) joke about my Monaghan Fianna Fáil background – and once took pleasure in correcting me for describing a place in Belfast as 'the Ardoyne'. That was British army style, he pointed out: locals never use the definite article, they just called it 'Ardoyne'.

But we shared an interest in Irish history, and I enjoyed discussing with him the relative merits of, say, Ernie O'Malley's and Tom Barry's accounts of the revolutionary years. 'You poor innocent', Michael Foley, sitting opposite, would lament at the spectacle of a mere interested amateur engaging Myers on one of his specialist subjects.

Once I found myself the unwitting catalyst for Kevin's polemical diary writing. The context was rugby: the 2001 British and Irish Lions (as they had become known from that year, having previously been the 'British Lions') tour of Australia, something for which I confessed little enthusiasm.

It was an 'anachronism', I thought, that in a Five or Six Nations championship, four of the 'home countries' should periodically gang up as one territory, to tour the former colonies. My distaste for the concept stemmed from attendance at part of the previous Lions tour in Australia, back in 1989, when a scoreboard in Sydney described the visitors as 'Great Britain', and when the only anthem used to represent them was 'God Save the Queen'.

On the other hand, then and now, I have always admired Irish rugby for fielding an all-Ireland team. And I'm sure that on this occasion, I also said (as I believe) that if Irish

involvement with the Lions was part of the price for
Northern unionists to play home games in Dublin and
endure 'The Soldier's Song' as an anthem, that was OK
by me.

So I was a little taken aback when, the next day, a
highly fictionalised version of both me and our conversation turned up in Kevin's 'Diary'. The piece was in general
a reflection on the confused identities of these islands, but
it began with this:

> 'It's an anachronism,' roared my friend Proinsias,
> who is from Ulster, where they are well acquainted
> with anachronisms: 'There's no reason whatever for
> players from this country to be playing in the same
> team as those … I think the word he used here was
> 'phuqquing', one I'm not acquainted with – Brits.
> 'It's an anachronism, so it is.'

I had certainly used the word 'anachronism' in our
conversation: that much was true. But I'm quite sure I
didn't say 'phuqquing', 'Brits', or 'so it is'. Also, I have
never roared anything in *The Irish Times*, then or since.
My opinions tend to be of the mildly held variety,
bordering on apologetic, which is why I never got into
the polemic business myself.

Then again, 'Proinsias' was a caricature, based only
very loosely on our conversation. Apart from us, no one
reading it would think the mad Ulsterman was me. And
I suppose this was a valuable insight into the methodology
of an opinion columnist, who on what may have been a
quiet day had picked up on a chance comment, turned it
into a wave of energy, and then surfed it for all it was
worth.

Despite such hiccups in our relationship, I was still on good terms with Kevin the last time we met. That must have been just before he moved out of Dublin to a new home in Kildare, because I remember expressing mock-serious concern on his behalf at the prospect of him becoming a remote worker.

'You need to come into the office and meet normal people like me,' I warned him. 'You'll lose the run of yourself completely out there among the horsey set.' This was a joke, mostly, but it had a half-serious point with which he agreed.

Yes, he said, journalists needed the company of other journalists. That's why he intended to work from the office a minimum of two days a week. But the resolution didn't last long, for whatever reason. By the time of the 1916 row, I hadn't seen him for at least two years. This added to his anger when I unwittingly misinformed the mutual correspondent about the reason for Kevin's absence from the paper.

His angry email caused me a sleepless night. Among other things, it accused me – along with most former colleagues – of not having picked up the phone to sympathise with him at the time of the 'MOBs' disaster when, as he said, he had suffered the worst attack on an Irish journalist in his lifetime.

And yes, it was true I hadn't considered calling him then. For one thing, he always seemed to thrive on notoriety: I had no way of knowing how traumatic he was finding this experience. But besides that, as I explained in a long, point-by-point reply, I had never flattered myself that I was a close friend of his and had never called him about anything else – nor he me. I was a junior colleague, who enjoyed talking to him in the office and occasionally the pub. That was the extent of our relationship.

He also claimed in his email that he was the only person from *The Irish Times* who had 'bothered' to turn up at my father's funeral. That was back in 1995, when I had been freelancing with the paper only a couple of years. And it wasn't quite accurate. Two other newsroom colleagues had made an appearance. But it's true that Kevin was there: a fact for which – as I told him in my reply – I was pathetically grateful.

Among my Dublin uncles and the few others present who read *The Irish Times* (the number by then included my mother), Myers's presence created a stir. It suggested I was a bigger success in Dublin journalism than was really the case.

I won't go into everything he said in the email, or my replies. But I finished by relaying something I had heard in the newsroom: that anyone with any influence over Kevin was being asked to try to persuade him to return. Again, I didn't flatter myself that he would listen. For what it was worth, however, I pleaded with him to change his mind.

It didn't work. He went ahead and joined *The Independent* anyway. Sometime after that, Geraldine called me into her office and said: 'You know what this is about, don't you?' I didn't, and guessed I was in trouble for some reason. When she asked me to take over the 'Diary', I was flabbergasted.

If it had once seemed like a dream job, it no longer did. The prospect filled me with dread. I had severe doubts whether I could write four columns of any kind a week, every week, never mind fill the previous incumbent's outsized shoes.

So I asked for a few days to think about it and Geraldine agreed. 'Don't take too long,' she warned: 'Eileen

Battersby wants it.' That sounded like a tactic to pressurise me into a quick yes, except that almost immediately, she took it back. 'But I'm not giving it to her,' she said.

While I was still reeling from the shock of being asked, others seemed to know about it already. Next day in the street, for example, I met my colleague Frank McDonald – a man nursing his own differences with management then – who had urgent advice.

'When they offer you the "Diary" job ...' he began, in a tone bordering on stern (I imagine him grabbing my lapel, but that probably didn't happen). The rest of his advice was stated in colourful language, but the gist of it was that I should demand an appropriate pay rise.

Unfortunately, on that theme, I had never asked for a rise in my life and, like most journalists, felt embarrassed whenever having to broach the subject of money. Also, by way of precedents, I had no idea what my predecessor earned, nor now could I ask him.

Instead, I asked my friend Alison O'Connor, a pragmatic Cork woman who had been staffed the same day as me and who now suggested I talk to Jack Fagan, the long-time Property Editor: 'He knows how everything works.' Sure enough, when asked what he thought Myers was earning, Fagan told me 'I'd be surprised if he was on less than [€x]'.

A day later, in the renewed meeting with the editor, I heard myself bring up the subject of my predecessor's salary and, with a shamelessness that surprised me, ventured: 'I'd be surprised if he was on less than [€x].' Geraldine didn't blink, saying only: 'But that was near the end of his career. You're still starting out.'

Feck, I thought to myself – that must have been an underestimate. And it wasn't quite true that I was just

144

starting out: I was already past 40 and the sole support of a wife and three children. But in the end we reached a compromise and, feeling like a financial genius, I secured the only unscheduled salary increase of my career, before or since.

The appointment as Irishman's Diarist was, in one way, literally, a non-event. For reasons still unclear it was never formally announced, with the usual picture and bio on page 3 that my mother and other proud relatives could cut out and keep.

Geraldine put a positive spin on this. 'I'm not going to announce you – we'll just let you take it over quietly,' she said. I wondered if this was an insurance policy against the risk of me proving an abject failure.

One day, a while later, I got a phone call from Paddy Prendiville of *The Phoenix*, inquiring if there was any truth in the rumour he or someone else had heard at a Dublin party – that all had been forgiven and Myers would be returning imminently to his old job. I told him it was the first I'd heard of it, which didn't mean it wasn't happening: 'I'd probably be the last to know.'

Paddy said he'd run the story anyway, and did. In keeping with my several *Phoenix* mentions around that time, it played up the contrast between Myers and the 'culchie comedian' who had replaced him.

In fairness, I played into that stereotype from the start. Determined to avoid comparisons with my predecessor, I also decided to write about what I knew, especially if it involved themes that the 'Diary' had not been strong on historically, including the GAA, rural life and the Ireland outside Dublin generally.

My debut column, therefore, was about the painful dilemma presented when my niece and goddaughter's

confirmation ceremony clashed directly with a first-round
Ulster Football Championship match between Monaghan
and Armagh.

It began like this:

I read somewhere that football is the new religion.
So when the Diocese of Clogher scheduled my
goddaughter's confirmation ceremony in direct opposition to last weekend's Ulster Championship
first-round game between Monaghan and Armagh,
it was fairly clear where my loyalties lay.

One of these events was a holy day of obligation;
the other was only a confirmation ceremony. Even
so, I hoped the church might remove any dilemma
for Monaghan supporters by rescheduling.

When it became clear that the old religion was
standing its ground, a second loophole opened.
Apparently, you don't need the full set of godparents
at a confirmation. Only one person accompanies the
confirmee to the altar, placing a hand on his or her
shoulder and silently vouching continued spiritual
guidance on the child's journey through life.

I knew that selection for this would be based
strictly on form. And sure enough, shortly beforehand, Aisling's parents had taken me aside and
explained gently that the godmother would be getting
the nod on this occasion. I'd be on the bench.

Did that mean I could go to Clones? No, it didn't.
It was made clear that I was still a valued squad
member. My absence might have an adverse effect
on team morale.

So I did what I had to do and made certain arrange-
ments. When the church proceedings began on

Sunday, I switched my mobile phone to silent and waited for the regular text messages promised by a fellow sect member at the game...

If there was ever a plot to bring Kevin Myers back from his Napoleonic exile in Abbey Street (where *The Independent* was still based then), as *The Phoenix* had speculated, it didn't come off. I became the resident Diarist for the next 19 years and counting. In the meantime, Kevin did not reply to my email. At the time of writing, I have not seen or heard from him since.

Baggage to Declare:
The Ups and Downs of Inheriting
a Century-old Newspaper Column

'THE IRISHMAN'S DIARY' FIRST APPEARED in the pages of *The Irish Times* in 1927, which may explain something about why it was so called.

Eighty years later, when I became the column's anchor tenant, it struck me as unfortunate that the name emphasised the writer's gender, something that had fallen out of fashion by then (especially if it was male). This was an accidental effect of the fact that, unlike, say, 'American' or 'German', there is no gender-neutral version of Irish ethnicity.

But it earned me the unwelcome attention of at least one of those latter-day social vigilantes: manel watchers. Manel watchers are more usually (and justifiably) exercised by ensuring equal representation for women on TV and radio panels, or in group pictures of people in public life.

So was my critic, who freely admitted that her main obsession was policing the man–woman ratio in press photographs. She had, however, noticed in passing the frequency with which the term 'Irishman's Diary' appeared in our pages, and this too had incurred her displeasure. She thought the column should be 'An Irishwoman's Diary' 50 per cent of the time (or, strictly speaking, 51, in proportion with demographic statistics).

I explained in vain that the Chief Diarist, of whatever gender, was contractually obliged to write the column four days a week. And although there was no reason the Chief

Diarist couldn't be female, it wasn't, for the moment: it was me.

In the era when women might have applied for the role – say from the 1960s onwards – the job had only become available twice. I was the second of those appointments (and it was made by a woman editor, the first in *Irish Times* history, Geraldine Kennedy).

On the days when the Chief Diarist wasn't writing it, I further explained, the 'Diary' was an equal-opportunity employer of casual contributors (chosen by the Letters Editor, not by me), at least in theory.

'So how many times has it been written by women?' the manel watcher wanted to know.

'Three thousand five hundred and forty-nine,' I shot back. Well, I didn't shoot, exactly: I had to search the phrase 'Irishwoman's Diary' in the archive to find that number. In the process, I was impressed to note that they stretched back to 1952.

This made the 'Diary' one of the first *Irish Times* features ever written by women, as I pointed out to our critic. But it was news to her that the column was written by women even now, because by her own admission, she never read it anyway.

This didn't prevent her having strong opinions about who wrote it. Unmoved by my defence, she still insisted it should be 'An Irishwoman's Diary' 51 per cent of the time.

Persistent as she may have been, it was not because of that critic that the column title did eventually undergo a partial name change in 2021. On the contrary, her argument for binary equality had become somewhat dated by then. It was only a matter of time before people started criticising the 'Irishman's/Irishwoman's' dichotomy as being unduly reductive of the complexity of human identity.

For that and other reasons, a decision was taken (corporately – I don't recall anyone asking my opinion, although I wouldn't have disagreed) to drop the gender reference altogether. Henceforth, the column would be simply 'An Irish Diary'.

But only online, not in the print edition. The logic there was that online readers were less likely to care about, or even be aware of, the newspaper's traditions.

Those include such things as page 'architecture' – for example the fact that, in the hard-copy newspaper, the 'Diary' has long occupied the same page as the editorials and Letters to the Editor, a point lost on most online readers but sacrosanct to those who buy the physical paper every day.

Out of respect for history, therefore, the column title remained unchanged in the print version (and of course in the e-paper, that being a facsimile of the hard copy). This classic compromise was not without confusion. After all, even some of *The Irish Times*'s biggest traditionalists now read the paper online too.

Hence a number of Letters to the Editor subsequently complaining about the de-gendering of the column's title. Those made perfect sense in the online edition. When they also appeared in the print version, however, they were lamenting the loss of the 'Irishman's Diary' title on the same page where it was still being used.

Even the new online title did not solve another problem I always had with the original: the question of why, in a paper called *The Irish Times*, we ever had to state explicitly that the Diarist was Irish. After all, most English-language newspapers and magazines have a column called simply 'Diary' or 'The Diary'.

This ranges from a miscellany of short items that don't

fit anywhere else (as in the London *Times*) to the guest 'Diary' of *The Spectator* magazine, where various celebrities take turns to describe a week in their fabulous lives.

The 1927 *Irish Times* version – also a miscellany of short, unrelated items – could have been just 'The Diary' too. But for a traditionally unionist newspaper, many of whose readers had considered themselves British as well as Irish and were now adjusting reluctantly to life in the Free State, it must have seemed a good idea to underline the ethnicity of its newest column.

Not everyone was impressed at this donning of the green jersey. The satirical magazine *Dublin Opinion*, for one, found the column's name an excuse to poke fun. In a 1930 full-page cartoon, it lampooned the *Irish Times* newsroom as a last bastion of the Anglo-Irish ascendancy, populated by Latin-speaking Oxbridge boffins, medal-wearing Colonel Blimps, mortarboard-hatted cleaning ladies discussing grammar, and various other species of West Briton.

The supposed exception was 'The Irishman's Diarist', depicted as occupying a corral of his own, not unlike a courthouse dock, with a peasant's caubeen on his head, a clay pipe in his pocket and a pig by his side. Even allowing for comic licence, this was very far from the reality of the 'Diary' then, which reflected the values of the old ascendancy at least as well as any other part of the newspaper.

The column in its early years revolved around hunt balls, yacht clubs and who was staying at the Shelbourne Hotel that week. One not untypical early item noted the 50th anniversary of the planting of a mulberry bush in the Trinity College Provost's garden, a stone's throw from the newspaper office.

The Irish Times's contributors then were typically Protestant Dubliners. So were the readers. In 1934, as recorded in his collected letters, a young Samuel Beckett – travelling in mainland Europe and trying to find himself – was being nagged by his family back in Foxrock to consider journalism: 'Mother writes why don't I contribute to the papers,' he confided to a friend at home. 'I write at least as well as the Irishman [*sic*] Diarist [she says].'

Whether Beckett ever did contribute to the 'Diary' is unknown (and unlikely). But by the time one Patrick Campbell began editing the column in the mid-1940s, plenty of other writers – both on *The Irish Times* payroll and beyond – did and were grateful for the guinea per item they were paid for what the paper's overall editor, Bertie Smyllie, once called 'lapidary crap'.

Tasked to improve the feature, Campbell first had to look up 'lapidary' in the dictionary (it means 'relating to the engraving or polishing of stones and gems'). Then, after his polishing of the regular contributors' work proved insufficient, he was invited to write it himself. This he did for a couple of years, turning the 'Diary' into a stylish and funny account of his own daily adventures, much to the chagrin of the former contributors, now robbed of their regular guineas.

But Campbell soon abandoned Dublin for London, where he was paid a lot more to write less. He also later became one of the first TV stars: turning his posh, Anglo-Irish accent and mild stammer into a selling point on the 1960s BBC panel show *Call My Bluff*.

His witty personal essays remain the standard most subsequent *Irish Times* Diarists tried to emulate, including me. At his best, he was a brilliant writer. Unfortunately, some years ago, I made the mistake of reading his autobiography,

My Life and Easy Times, and ended up hating everything else about him. The book's title was a joking play on James Thurber's memoir *My Life and Hard Times*. Joke or not, however, *My Life and Easy Times* was also an all-too-accurate summary of Campbell's career.

He was a son of the old Ascendancy whose path through life had been smoothed at every turn by his aristocratic father, Lord Glenavy. The young Patrick went to an English public school, then Oxford (briefly), before his old man's pull got him a job in *The Irish Times*.

'The Lord' (as Glenavy is referred to in the memoir) then provided an entrée into London journalism. But having left Dublin for the bigger money of Fleet Street, Campbell Jr returned home in a hurry in 1939, before he might have had to fight for England, bribing his way onto the last ferry out of Liverpool. An experienced yachtsman, he spent the Emergency (the official designation of the war years in neutral Ireland) patrolling Dublin Port against the small risk of U-boats.

In 1944, boredom drove him to prostrate himself before Smyllie and ask for his old job back, which was reluctantly granted. Then two years later, he abandoned it again, this time for good.

During hist first stint with the newspaper, Campbell had been the Dáil sketch writer, as which one of the things he enjoyed doing was sending up the accents and speech mannerisms of certain rural Fianna Fáil TDs. No doubt they deserved it, sometimes.

But in mocking them, Campbell also played up to the relatively urbane Fine Gael deputies he considered his equals (or nearly), whose better contributions he highlighted:

Some of the brighter and more ambitious members of the Dáil began to appreciate it, too, particularly on the Fine Gael side. It became a habit with them, after a specially sharp passage of invective at the expense of the Government, to glance up to see if I'd got it.

I invented an expression to show that I had – a slightly cynical half-smile, and a casual jotting in my notebook.

It was the first taste of power I'd ever had. It was warming and relaxing. It was very good indeed.

Perhaps it was oversensitivity on behalf of my own rural Fianna Fáil forebears, but that just sounds insufferably˙ smug now. Reading it and Campbell's other if-he-was-chocolate-he'd-eat-himself moments made me reach for the sick bucket.

Another thing I struggle to forgive him for is that he somehow managed to write a memoir of his *Irish Times* years, including the mid-1940s, without mentioning Brian O'Nolan, aka Flann O'Brien and (under his journalist's caubeen) Myles na gCopaleen.

A flawed but nevertheless much greater writer than Campbell, Myles was at his brilliant best in the first half of the 1940s, when his hilarious 'Cruiskeen Lawn' column often shared a page with the 'Diary'. It was arguably that era's funniest column in the English language. But not only does Campbell fail to mention it in the memoir, he gives as one of the excuses for leaving the paper a second time the reasoning that he had 'no competition' there.

Contrary to a popular misconception, Myles himself never wrote the 'Diary'. To the best of my knowledge, his only appearance within its precincts was a case of breaking and entering one day in 1943. In a typically elaborate joke, he arranged with the page editor to breach the party wall between the two columns and allow him invade the neighbouring one, briefly, for a 'change of air'.

This was taking up where the *Dublin Opinion* cartoon left off, except that Myles depicted the 'Diary' as an extreme example of the newspaper's upper-class values. After mock-admiring the civilised atmosphere around him for a paragraph, he withdrew again, back to his own corral.

And yet the parallel histories of 'Cruiskeen Lawn' and 'An Irishman's Diary' are still often confused, even in *The Irish Times*. When the paper produced an e-book of my columns a few years ago, a blurb I've never had the heart to amend linked me flatteringly with 'the original Diarist Myles na gCopaleen'.

A few years later, visiting a bar called The Irish Times in Tokyo in 2019, I was amused to see that among the painted-on smoke stains and other fake-authentic fittings of a typical mid-twentieth-century Dublin pub was a framed legend proclaiming 'Myles na gCopaleen – An Irishman's Diary'.

Oh well. If 'Cruiskeen Lawn' died with Myles in 1966, its spirit lives on still, in the 'Diary' and elsewhere. For anyone attempting to be funny in *The Irish Times*, he is the giant at your shoulder. Patrick Campbell is comparatively forgotten.

The sombrero-wearing, opera-singing Smyllie himself – one of Dublin's great eccentrics of the 1940s – was also a regular Diarist for years, writing the slot once a week under the nom de plume 'Nichevo'.

But for decades, the column's usual pseudonym was 'Quidnunc' (when written by a man) and 'Candida' (when a woman). The best-known Candida was Eileen O'Brien, who also wrote it once a week for many years. By far the longest-running Quidnunc, meanwhile – chief writer from the late 1940s to the 1970s – was Seamus Kelly, an ex-army officer now immortalised by a bust in the newspaper's front lobby.

It was only when Kevin Myers became the regular writer in the early 1980s that the old pseudonyms were finally dropped and personal bylines became the norm.

Since taking over the job in 2006, I have tried to learn from all my predecessors. I have also stolen from most of them on occasion. And despite my misgivings about Campbell's personality, I did learn at least one useful thing from his biography: never to try to build up a reserve of columns.

Once, haunted by a dream in which the newspaper appeared with a blank space where his diary should be, Campbell filed an extra piece to be used in emergencies, when inspiration or his nerve failed him.

Then, between early and late editions one night, an editor noticed this 'spare' lying around, decided it was better than the one already gone to print, and substituted it for the later 'city' edition. Thus, two of the Diarist's hard-earned columns were used up on the same day. He never made that mistake again.

But to be strictly honest, I didn't so much learn that lesson from Campbell as use it for retrospective validation of what, until then, I had considered a bad habit of my own. Frequently over the years, *Irish Times* colleagues or interested readers have inquired of me how many future columns I keep stockpiled at any given time. The terrible truth, always, is none.

Since my first day in the job, 17 May 2006, I have

invariably written today for tomorrow. The only advance in two decades, as several long-suffering sub-editors can testify, is that my average time for filing copy has become slightly later with every year.

The Stony Grey Soil of Dalkey: Poetic Justice in the High Court

IF I WAS FORCED TO nominate a favourite among my 3,700 (and counting) Irishman's Diaries, it might be one from April 2008.

This is in part because it wasn't really mine at all. I suspect it was ghost-written by the poet Patrick Kavanagh, possibly with help from another of my literary heroes, Myles na gCopaleen (aka Flann O'Brien).

For me, as for all Monaghan people, Kavanagh's influence has always been impossible to ignore, even if you try. Everywhere you go in Ireland, when people of a certain age find out where you're from, you hear the same three words, often the only thing they can remember about Monaghan: 'Stony grey soil'.

But I have inhaled deeply of Kavanagh's other poems too, and know quite a few by heart. I'm intimately connected not just with the border drumlin country of his early work but also with the part of Dublin he frequented most of his adult life: in and around Baggot Street, where, as Benedict Kiely said, an exiled Kavanagh recreated the main street of fair-day Carrickmacross.

A line from 'On Raglan Road', his great if flawed ballad (I love the first two verses, not so much the rest) spoke to me too. Sitting in Bewley's of Grafton Street on my first summer in Dublin, feeling a little lost, I could lament with feeling: 'The Queen of Hearts still making tarts and I not making hay.'

Kavanagh and Brian O'Nolan (the real-life Flann and Myles) were good friends, after an awkward start. When the poet's 'Spraying the Potatoes' was published in *The Irish Times* in 1940, O'Nolan and his city-slicker circle of ex-UCD pals satirised it in some of their many prank letters to the newspaper.

Kavanagh didn't take this personally. Instead, he responded with the intellectual sophistication that lurked – well hidden until then – under his public posture as a peasant poet.

The fake letters, enormously popular with *Irish Times* readers, helped earn O'Nolan his own daily column in the paper later that year. In the meantime, he learned to be more respectful of Kavanagh and never underestimated him again.

They were sometimes wary friends, but friends nonetheless. Kavanagh quarrelled with just about every other writer in Dublin at one time or another (including the dead W.B. Yeats, who was one of his chief enemies), but not, it seems, with Myles.

Much as I love their work, I'm glad I never met either man. My former colleague Nuala O'Faolain, who did, recalled seeing Myles in a Dublin bar in the 1960s, very drunk, and urinating against the counter.

Both men were severe alcoholics in later years, although Kavanagh's perennial shortage of money (Brendan Behan called him 'the Monaghan toucher' for his tendency to seek loans) restrained his drinking habits somewhat.

Still, they live on – and are perhaps best encountered – in their writings. This is the only place I knew them, at least until one morning in 2008. I was, as usual, stuck for ideas to fill the next day's column. Also as usual, with a deadline looming, the anxiety in the pit of my stomach was gradually giving way to panic.

Then I found myself reading the latest reports on a

court case involving a land dispute in Dalkey, the affluent south Dublin suburb. It was in most ways a very ordinary Irish row between neighbours, in this case over a piece of scrubland called Gorse Hill.

Except that one of the parties involved was Pat Kenny, the TV and radio star, so there was huge public attention to the case. Despite this, it had passed me by, until that morning, reading a description of the disputed land, a phrase from my Leaving Cert poetry floated before me: 'Half a rood of rock'.

And with that, a fully formed column fell into my laptop. It was as if Kavanagh and Myles, peering over my shoulder, had pushed me aside and said: 'Move over there, sonny. Let us have a go.' So I did.

Here's what they wrote (contrary to what it says in the text, I was nowhere near the courtroom that week):

He seems to have gone unnoticed amid the general obsession with Pat Kenny. But among the more unusual visitors to the Dalkey land dispute case at the High Court this week has been the ghost of Patrick Kavanagh.

I spotted him straight away, the first morning. In fact, I had no choice. He stood on my foot with his size-12 hobnailed boots as he shuffled past me in the packed public gallery, searching for a non-existent seat. And it was reassuring to see him, despite the pain, if only because he eased my own guilt about being there.

There seemed no justifiable reason for attending the case, other than pure nosiness. I had just happened to be passing when I saw the media scrum outside, and couldn't resist dropping in for a few minutes.

But the feeling of prurience was still nagging me when Kavanagh appeared.

Then I remembered his famous sonnet, 'Epic', and its opening lines: 'I have lived in important places, times/ When great events were decided: who owned/ That half a rood of rock, a no-man's land/ Surrounded by our pitchfork-armed claims.'

The similarities between the Gorse Hill saga and the events Kavanagh described were striking. In fairness, there have been no pitchforks used in Dalkey (not that we've heard yet, anyway). And at 0.2 acres, the disputed piece of rock there is closer to three-quarters of a rood than a half.

Also, on a technical point, there are no 'gorse hills' in Kavanagh Country, only hills covered with 'whins'. But still, the resemblances between the two scenarios were uncanny. They became more so when counsel spoke of raised fists, angry words, gates being closed on people's arms, and so on.

Another verse from the poem came back to me: 'I heard the Duffys shouting "Damn your soul"/ And old McCabe, stripped to the waist, seen/ Step the plot defying blue cast-steel — / "Here is the march along these iron stones".'

I noticed Kavanagh taking copious notes, no doubt for use in a future poem. And yet it was hard to imagine how the evidence would help him improve on his original, unless he were simply to relocate the action from Inniskeen to suburban south Dublin.

This might be useful, in fact. I have since discovered that, in its poetry notes for students, a popular education website cites the lines 'That half a rood of rock, a no-man's land/ Surrounded by our pitchfork-armed claims' as an example of – and I quote: 'the loneliness, conflicts, and frustrations of rural life'.

Fair enough. But it may be worth reminding Dublin kids that, despite their rugby schools and their hoity-toity lifestyles, they are not necessarily above this sort of thing. If the High Court case serves any useful purpose, it shows that the themes of 'Epic' are universal, not just applicable to muck savages from Monaghan.

Of course, Kavanagh makes this point himself when he recalls, in the poem's conclusion, that the Duffy/McCabe row happened in 1938, as supposedly greater events were unfolding elsewhere:

'That was the year of the Munich bother. Which/ Was most important? I inclined/ To lose my faith in Ballyrush and Gortin/ Till Homer's ghost came whispering to my mind./ He said: I made the *Iliad* from such/ A local row. Gods make their own importance.'

Yes, this is the real message of the Dalkey case for we mortals: that not even the gods are immune from neighbourly tensions. That, on the contrary, passionate boundary disputes can just as easily occur in the vicinity of Mount Olympus (or Killiney Hill, as it's known in Dublin).

I didn't see Homer's ghost in the public gallery, by the way. But I could easily have missed him. The case is being heard in the High Court's new rooms at the Distillery Building, and I've heard there are spirits all over the place in there. (It's not true, however, that juries hearing cases on the premises can reach verdicts on the basis of 40 per cent proof; although I have previously proposed such a reform as a means of reducing the courts' backlog.)

Anyway, reassured that my presence in the gallery was motivated by more than vulgar curiosity, but was rather an exercise in better understanding mankind, I sat through all the gory details that the lawyers insisted on revealing. And when the hearing finally ended, I waited at the door for a chance to meet my hero. No, not Pat Kenny. Kavanagh, I mean.

I was a bit nervous, given his fierce reputation. But I remembered that in another poem, he once invited us: 'If ever you go to Dublin town, in a hundred years or so, inquire for my ghost on Baggot Street ...' The specified period had not elapsed, I knew, and this was the wrong part of town. Even so, I hoped to find him in a mellow mood.

I was not disappointed. No doubt buoyed by the evidence that 'Epic' was holding its relevance so well 70 years after the events that inspired it, he was in the best of form. So when I blurted out something about how his poetry had touched all our lives, he thanked me warmly, shook my hand, and went on his way.

Then he paused and turned to me again. 'Speaking of being touched,' he said. 'Any chance you could lend me a few bob?'

A day after the piece appeared, I received a postcard from Tom Stack, a Dublin Jesuit priest who loved Kavanagh's poetry and had written a book about him. He knew Pat Kenny well too and, meeting him that morning, told me they had shared a laugh over the column. So that was nice.

But the cherry on the cake was a letter to *The Irish Times* from Tim Magennis (a remarkable man in his own right, who in the mid-1960s, became the first and still only Irishman to sail around the world under something called 'gaff rig').

The letter read: 'We have had to wait a long time for an Irish Times column that offered just a little flavour of Myles na Gopaleen at his best but Frank McNally, bless him, has done it with his splendid piece on Patrick Kavanagh, Pat Kenny and the Dalkey land dispute.'

If only my ghost writers had turned up more often over the years, life as the Irishman's Diarist would have been a lot easier. I should probably have quit then, while I was still ahead.

Dream

IT'S PROBABLY A COMMON AFFLICTION among journalists – I must ask at the next group therapy meeting. But for many years now, I've had this recurring dream, bordering on nightmare, involving deadlines. It's always set late in the evening and I'm out on assignment somewhere, with a long, complicated news feature to file imminently.

For often unexplained reasons, however, I haven't started writing the piece yet. Nor, for reasons that are also usually unclear – but that might include mere procrastination – *can* I start, despite mounting anxiety about the shortness of time remaining.

These problems are never resolved, one way or another. I never get around to writing the piece and the deadline never passes. In fact, nothing much happens in the dream except that it gets later and later, and the deadline fear grows.

Finally, I wake up and think: Thank God! That wasn't real! Then the knot in my stomach unwinds and I breathe a deep sigh of relief. The ordeal is almost worth it for this. No matter how stressful the day ahead seems, the sense of reprieve makes it a good morning.

Some years ago, in a place that shall remain nameless, the dream almost came to life. It was the first night of a General Election campaign, and I had to accompany one of the party leaders' buses on a tour of rural towns that ended with this one, where the last speech of the day was scheduled.

This left me with a choice. Option one: I could stay on the bus, which had good Wi-Fi, and write up my feature on the way back to Dublin. The drawback with that was nausea. Even reading on a bus makes me feel sick, never mind trying to type as well.

So after catching a bit of the last speech, I went with option two: to go to a local hotel instead and work from there, taking my chances afterwards with public transport. There were regular buses and trains back to Dublin, I knew. But when the deadline fear is upon you, the risk of getting stuck somewhere overnight can be a secondary concern.

Anyway, as in the dream, I did indeed have a longish piece to write, and about half the time ideally required for it. On the way to the hotel, the gnawing-in-the-pit-of-my-stomach phase was well advanced. The cold sweat phase wasn't far off.

As usual back then, uncertainty about whether the hotel would have good (or any) Wi-Fi added to the general anxiety. But before I could find out about the Wi-Fi, as always happens in the dream too, something mysterious intervened.

At the entrance to the hotel, I was approached by a woman who drew my attention to an elderly man leaning against the wall nearby, and asked if I could help him down the street. 'He only lives around the corner,' she said, 'but I can't do it.' With that, she was gone.

It was a deft move on her part, I thought afterwards. Her words conveyed deep empathy for the man's plight and made it sound unthinkable that anyone would choose not to help him. But without explaining why she couldn't do it, she had transferred all this on to me. Suddenly, he was my problem.

I studied him a moment, hoping he was merely drunk, in which case I could excuse myself with a clear conscience. But he wasn't drunk. He was just old and frail. Even with the help of a walking stick, he was struggling to stay on his feet.

So of course, I offered to help. And thanking me, he gripped my arm. 'I'm only round the corner,' he said, echoing the woman's words. Then he started walking. Very slowly. I mean – really, really, slowly. No, reader: even slower than that.

It would be an exaggeration to say that the man walked at a snail's pace, but not much of an exaggeration. Each of his steps was only an inch or two, yet it took such an effort for him he also had pause for rest between every three or four to regather his energy.

Even as I noticed this, I also noticed for the first time that the nearest corner – the one he supposedly lived just around – was not all that near. Furthermore, I now began to experience intense concern about what the phrase 'just around the corner' might mean. With this, the gnawing in my stomach grew.

Thanking me again, the old man proceeded to list his various medical problems. It was a long list, including arthritis and thrombosis and I can't remember what else. Then he mentioned that he should have called an ambulance earlier when he was leaving wherever he'd been. So, already in search of an exit strategy, I grasped at this and offered to call an ambulance for him now.

But no, he wouldn't hear of that. 'I'll be grand once I'm home,' he insisted. Nor would he let me phone a taxi, although I'd gladly have paid for one. 'It's only a hundred yards,' he said.

We had travelled maybe 20 of his miniature steps by this point. My frustration was such that I had taken to urging him onwards physically, pushing his arm as if hoping that the rest of him might sprout castors, like a suitcase.

Painfully aware of the time elapsing, I decided to appeal to his conscience and explain my situation. Doing this, I used words like 'story', 'deadline' and 'news-desk will kill me'. But even as these jargon terms came out of my mouth, I could sense they were meaningless to him. They sounded a bit foreign to me too, suddenly.

He didn't even seem to hear them, anyway. If he did, he pretended otherwise. 'I'm only round the corner,' he said again. 'We're nearly there.'

We were not nearly there. I was now considering such options as saying: 'I'm really sorry, but...' and running away. Then he started telling me about how somebody had passed him earlier and promised to return, but didn't: 'I've known him all me life, but if I was to wait until next week, he wouldn't come back. It's terrible how quick people you think are your friends desert you.'

Hearing this, my heart sank. The temptation to do a runner died of shame. Even so, I found myself wondering if, despite his apparent distress, this journey was a routine occurrence that neighbours, like those even now hurrying past us, had learned to avoid.

Panic rising, I asked if there was a family member I could ring for help. There was, he said. My heart lifted anew. Unfortunately, he couldn't remember the phone number. He recited the first three digits – I was pressing them even as he spoke – then went blank.

Foiled again, I offered to run around to the house and ask whoever was there to come and meet him. 'It's just that I'm under a bit of time pressure,' I explained. And, although clearly reluctant to let me go, he now gave me the directions. Memorising which, with relief and guilt, I propped him against a parked car and sprinted for the corner.

As feared, nothing around the corner quite resembled what he had just said. I tried the address on a passer-by. Blank look. Then I saw a shop and ran to that, where the assistant pointed me back the way I'd come.

It turned out that, in a fog of stress, I had bypassed the slightly hidden entrance. The street really was just around the corner, or near enough. When I found his house, though, there seemed to be no lights on anywhere. This too was like something from the dream.

Knocking on the door dubiously, I was already thinking of plan B – ringing the ambulance after all – when a woman answered. It was his daughter, I guessed. And hearing the story, she just nodded with a resigned air. This had happened before, no doubt. But relieved to have offloaded the responsibility, I ran back to the man and told him help would be arriving shortly.

Then I mentioned 'deadlines' again, wished him well, and left. God love him, his living nightmare was more serious than mine. Not that this was any comfort at the time.

Back at the hotel again, out of breath, I finally got around to asking the receptionist if they had Wi-Fi. Yes they had, he said. Unfortunately, it wasn't working. Of course. Nothing ever works in the dream, either.

Then I inquired where else nearby might have it and still be open at this time. The man on the desk thought hard and suggested a certain café that might. But he didn't sound confident.

The gnawing in my stomach worsened as I inquired where the café was. The address meant nothing to me. Which direction was that, I asked. At which point, just as would happen in the dream, the man pointed vaguely towards somewhere in the darkness on the edge of town ...

Of course, if it really *had* been a dream, I would have woken up around then and thought: Thank God! Alas, this was real life.

There was a time in my early years in journalism when, if technology failed you – as it did often – you always had the fall-back of phoning your story in to the copy-takers. There were only two or three left by then. But they were very good and efficient, able to type your story up almost as quick as you could read it. They were all female too, and their soothing tones added to the relief if you'd been having a stressful experience.

One excruciating night in Cobh, in the mid-1990s, when Irish Steel seemed to have closed (it had a temporary reprieve soon afterwards), I had to find a landline somewhere that I could plug my laptop into to file my 'colour piece' electronically.

There was no Wi-Fi at that time. But as I hadn't yet realised, there was a fault in the computer that wouldn't allow it to send stuff even via a landline. In the meantime, one of my failed attempts involved a phone behind the counter of a friendly pub, the owner of which allowed me to disconnect it long enough to plug my laptop in and dial up the internet.

The socket happened to be down at floor level. So there I was, in a cold sweat, down on my hand and knees waiting for the reassuring crackle and dial tone that meant deliverance. It never came. In the meantime, a drunken customer on a stool nearby patted my bottom. Yes, #MeToo, reader.

When I rang tech support in *The Irish Times*, they

suggested various fixes (for the laptop, not the drunken customer), none of which worked. They were always reluctant to give in and let you resort to the copy-takers: that represented failure of the new technology. But as I phoned my piece in to Deirdre, eventually, her soft voice was like that of a therapist, and much needed.

Alas, the copy-takers had gone the way of the Mohicans by the time of that night on the election trail. So, giving up on the search for working Wi-Fi locally, I cut my losses and legged it back to the campaign bus, which still hadn't left town.

High on adrenaline, I wrote up my piece on the way back to Dublin after all, the journey passing unnoticed until I hit 'send' and looked up to see we were almost in the city centre. Sure enough, I was feeling nauseous. But luckily, I'd been too stressed to notice until then.

***

Even the word 'deadline' sounds ominous, and so it should, given its history. When journalists like me resort to hyperbole about it, as we do, and especially when we talk about how we need a 'gun to the head' to get anything done, as we also do, we really shouldn't. Because the origins of the term are deadly enough already.

It was as two words that it first became popularised, during the American Civil War. Back then, the 'dead line' was a notional boundary inside or outside the official perimeter of a military internment camp, where they hadn't got around to erecting fences yet. Sometimes it comprised nothing more than a low rail, rope or trench. But a prisoner who crossed it, or even threatened to cross, risked being shot. Typically, he was.

According to the Merriam-Webster dictionary, the phrase began to appear in print circa 1863, including one example – in a letter to a Tennessee newspaper – that was already borrowing it for figurative use. Its appearances multiplied in 1864 thanks to one especially notorious prison in Confederate Georgia. Built to house 10,000 inmates, Andersonville Prison had 26,000 by the war's end, despite appalling death tolls – 100 a day at one point – from disease, malnutrition and cruelty.

The camp commandant, Swiss-born Henry Wirz, was later hanged for war crimes, one of only two people to achieve that distinction in the US Civil War. His camp was largely responsible for popularising the term 'dead line', via official reports, early histories of the war and poetry.

A Sanitary Commission Bulletin of September 1864 explained the concept as follows: 'Twenty feet inside and parallel to the fence is a light railing, forming the "dead line," beyond which the projection of a foot or finger is sure to bring the deadly bullet of the sentinel.'

An anti-slavery Boston newspaper, *The Liberator*, expressed the grim reality in verse: 'No shelter know the sufferers; bolder ones / Daring to seek it, scorched by the Georgian suns, / Drop on the dead-line 'neath the warders' guns.'

Faced with the horrors of the camps, some inmates preferred to die. Thomas Prentice Kettell's *History of the Great Rebellion* (1866) records an army memo sent to Abraham Lincoln about the Andersonville prisoners' plight:

They are fast losing hope and becoming utterly reck-less of life. Numbers, crazed by their sufferings, wander about in a state of idiocy. Others deliberately cross the 'Dead Line' and are remorselessly shot down.

Although 'deadline' was used as a metaphor during and immediately after the Civil War, it took half a century or more for the euphemism to enter the mainstream.

The medium then was journalism, but not the subject. Instead, the image was being borrowed by death's jovial companion in inevitability – taxes. Returns at that point had to be in by 1 January. Hence a newspaper article of 30 December 1919, predicting a flood of petitions over-night given the imminent 'deadline for filings'.

**

In the light of such grisly origins, the mere stresses faced by journalists under time pressure are minor sufferings.

Unfortunately, this is never much help to the daily or weekly columnist staring at a blank screen as the deadline looms. Or to the late-night reporter, haunted by the hole in the newspaper that awaits imminent filling.

For those of us who both require deadlines to function and yet are terrorised by them to the extent that they invade our dreams, the worst possible career move may be to become an accidental, part-time sports reporter. This is exactly what happened to me.

Apart from a few schools' rugby games back in my freelancing days, I have never worked for the official sports department of any media organisation. The general newsroom was usually my home. But I like most sports. And so, over the years, I gained the reputation as someone who could write about them with feeling, if the need arose.

In *The Irish Times*, for years, whenever a sporting event transcended the sports section, being deemed worthy of a slot in the news pages – maybe even on the front page – I was the go-to person to write it. The job did not call for a sports report, exactly. What they wanted was 'colour': a breezy news piece conveying the atmosphere around the event, the mood of the fans and any other quirky tangents that might entertain readers.

But the big football matches, especially, tend to be at night, kicking off at 7.45pm and ending precariously close to the time when the first editions of print newspapers go 'to bed'. That's when the colour happened too. When you're capturing the mood of fans, after all, the game itself is all-important. Yes, you try to 'bank' a few paragraphs in advance: a funny story about the extremes someone went to in order to attend, for example. Or the price of tickets being charged by touts. Or the weather.

Weather can be crucial. 'It was a dark and stormy night' is a famously bad way to start a novel. But for a colour writer at a World Cup qualifying match, it's a great nerve settler. Meteorological drama – the more violent the better – is your friend then. Not only will it give you several easy paragraphs in advance, it oftens provides a useful metaphor that can be adapted to suit the game itself.

But the outcome – win, lose or draw – is still everything. And the problem with trying to write a definitive colour piece about the Irish soccer team, especially (at least back in the days when we were good), is that the outcome was rarely obvious until the final whistle.

The typical Irish performance for years involved us going a goal down early on to superior opposition who threatened to overwhelm us, then battling back bravely and snatching an equaliser in the dying minutes, so that the 1–1 draw felt like a moral victory. This was expressed in the infamous chant: 'You'll never beat the Irish'. Which carried the implicit message that the Irish wouldn't beat you either, but that when we salvaged a draw against the odds, we would then celebrate as if we had.

This could be gut-wrenching for supporters. For newspaper colour writers, trying to sum up the match in ways that might appear elegant and witty to someone reading the next day's paper, it could be horrible. Full-time sports reporters develop strategies to deal with the problem, writing up games as they go, a paragraph at a time, then putting a 'top' on it after the final whistle. That didn't work so well for colour pieces.

Besides, while I did this often over the years, it was never often enough to cope well with the stress. There have been occasions near the end of games when, with the deadline minutes away, I was incapable of having a coherent thought, never mind expressing it in elegant sentences.

Sometimes the idea of actual death – preferably immediate and painless, from the bullet of some invisible sentry guard who'd caught me stepping over the dead line – seemed a comforting alternative to the reality.

***

Sports writers are often accused of being 'fans with typewriters', wearing their hearts on team-coloured sleeves and lacking the objectivity expected of other journalists. I can empathise with that. Whenever Ireland play, I generally want them to win, even if I'm sitting in a press box and pretending detachment.

If it's a late-night game, however, or the deadline is

otherwise tight enough to provoke dread, I become miraculously cured of any nationalistic fervour. My sole hope then is that our fate – good or bad – will be known as early as possible, so that I can get on with being witty and elegant about the outcome. Should this mean Ireland being outclassed from the kick-off and the game being effectively over by half-time, well, sorry, but that's so much less nerve-wracking than covering our more usual doomed heroics.

One infamous night back in October 2012, I had to write the front-page colour piece on a World Cup qualifier between Ireland and Germany. The next day's print edition was exceptionally large, I think, or we had a bigger-than-normal print run. Either way, early copy was more than usually important.

This led to a news editor (who may have had previous experience of me, in the technical journalistic phrase) 'tearing the arse out of' my deadline, dispensing orders of military-style strictness. I was to file most of my report – all but the opening paragraph – by 9.10pm at the latest. The intro I could add five minutes after the full-time whistle. Or, the editor added, in what sounded like a veiled threat, the News Desk would add that for me.

These strictures were of course offensive to my inner artist. By 9.10pm, the game would be at best about 20 minutes into the second half. It was like asking James Joyce to write 90 per cent of 'The Dead' without knowing what Gretta Conroy was going to say about Michael Furey back in the hotel room, and to fill that bit in five minutes after it happened.

Anyway, as the game kicked off, my nerves were frayed even more than usual. I banked a few paragraphs about the pipe band that played the national anthem and about Ireland coach Giovanni Trapattoni's programme notes.

Then I hoped against hope that, for once, the result might become obvious early.

Great was my secret relief when, after half an hour of brave Irish defending, the Germans scored twice in quick succession. A comeback from there, while possible, was unlikely. By half-time, I could safely describe Ireland as having been plucky but outclassed.

When Germany added two more goals, early in the second half, I tried to look as grave-faced as anyone else in the press box, while performing mental cartwheels and thanking God – obviously a Lutheran, I now believed – for this unexpected intervention. There was no way Ireland were coming back from this. My 9.10pm dispatch could now be definitive about how outclassed we were – I just had to take out the bits about us being 'plucky'.

Having trouble with the stadium Wi-Fi, I abandoned the press box to file the preliminary dispatch. By the time I got down to the media centre, in the bowels of the stadium, the score was 0–5. Now my only concern was that I had not fully reflected the scale of what was becoming a national disaster. I took out a few qualifying adjectives, made the language more stark, and hit 'send'.

On the way back up in the lift, Lutheran God even gave me a funny story as a bonus. The lift operator showed me a betting docket whereon he had Ireland to lose 0–5 and 1–6, backing each scoreline for a fiver at 100–1.

But when I congratulated him on being right (so far) about the 0–5, the man was despondent. 'They're going to win 6 or 7 nil,' he said. Sure enough, back in my seat, I watched the Germans add another. Then – Lo! – Ireland scored a late consolation that meant nothing, except to the man in the lift for whom it won €500.

I was almost as happy for him as for myself. Rarely

can the humiliation of one's own team have made for such contentment as I felt that night. Yes, I knew this was traitorous. So, like everyone else in the press box, I maintained a glum face, while quietly luxuriating in the five minutes after full time in which I could top off the piece:

Halloween came early at the Aviva Stadium last night when the ghoulies and ghosties and long-legged beasties of the German national football team treated home fans to their scariest 90 minutes in living memory.

The 6–1 scoreline was Ireland's worst ever competitive home defeat. Only a last-minute goal by Andy Keogh averted total humiliation, although before that went in, we were lucky to be on nil.

It began well at least. In what was surely a first for an Irish soccer manager, Giovanni Trapattoni quoted the German philosopher Nietzsche in his programme notes, saying of his team's Euro 2012 debacle: 'What doesn't kill you makes you stronger.'

The theme appeared to be taken up by the stadium PA, which welcomed the teams on to the pitch to the strains of 'Thus Spoke Zarathustra'.

But this only seemed to be asking for trouble against the Germans. And sure enough, after taking a few minutes to acclimatise, the visitors soon established themselves as the Übermensch …

I'm not sure what would happen if you failed to file an expected piece with the newspaper as a whole up against deadline. The question does cross your mind on occasion.

You imagine having a heart attack from the stress or

having to tell an editor: 'Sorry, my nerves have gone – I can't do this any more.' I suppose, if it was the front page, they'd have to do a quick redesign and make the lead picture bigger, or something.

The nearest I've been to finding out had nothing to do with stress, strange to say. It was the opposite. One night in our Belfast office, in the days before or after the Good Friday Agreement, a colleague and I were jointly writing a news piece for one of the inside pages.

It was finished, but between the two of us, we somehow forgot to hit send. Then, post-deadline relaxation set in and we were having a chat, blissfully unaware of the panic back on the News Desk in Dublin until the phone rang with a desperate editor at the other end.

Red-faced, we sent the story belatedly and it made the first edition as planned. But the man on the desk chastened us later by saying how close we'd been to the dreaded hole in the page. There wasn't even a substitute story he could have slotted in, apparently.

'I was on the point of having to put an ad there instead,' he confessed with horror.

Plan B in Operation:
A Surprise Double
7 July 2005

INVADING THE PITCH AT CROKE Park last Sunday, I was alarmed to hear the PA announcing a coded message: 'Plan B in operation!' For a terrible moment, I thought they were going to shoot the Monaghan supporters who had run onto the field.

Instead, stewards reacted to the announcement by surrendering to the invasion. They even started helping people over the barriers, clearly realising that some of us were out of practice.

Plan A, presumably, was to prevent a pitch incursion (in what must have seemed the unlikely event that anyone would get excited about winning the National Football League Division Two Championship).

But the miraculous nature of the victory – by a goal from a Hail-Mary free kick in the game's last moment – produced an outpouring of joy that neither Monaghan hearts nor plan A could contain.

Instead, the GAA chose the life-affirming option of letting us enjoy a rare moment in the sun. And the sun really did shine as the winning captain delivered a speech worthy of an All-Ireland Final, vowing that the team would be back again here soon, for bigger things.

Incredibly, Monaghan's victory was not the only small miracle I had witnessed that week. The first was arguably bigger – weighing in at 8lb 7oz. And he too had provoked an outpouring of joy among the (somewhat smaller) attendance at the National Maternity Hospital on Thursday night.

When doctors handed him to me, I felt like making a speech – thanking the selectors, the sponsors, my mother and father, and so on. But I somehow restrained myself, because my wife might have been traumatised by the bit where I vowed we'd be back here again on the third weekend in September.

The truth is some of us were out of practice at this sort of thing too. It was sobering to recall that our existing children both dated from the late twentieth century. We'd got used to having just the two, and for various reasons thought that might be it.

So amid the excitement of learning that there was another on the way, I had to make some adjustments as well. It was as if there was a little PA announcer in my head saying: 'Plan B in operation!'

This one was a whole new experience. For one thing, there were two small people that needed to be briefed first.

The reaction of Patrick, aged five, who was finally about to lose his title of baby-in-residence, was particularly important. Luckily, he was very mature about the pregnancy, with the minor qualification that, if it were a girl, he would 'put her in the bin'.

We laughed nervously at that, while making a mental note to hide all sharp objects when the new child arrived. Roisín (six) was less of a worry, except that, whatever the baby's gender, she was planning to put dresses on it.

The other novelty was that the impending arrival was coming the wrong way round and, like a small Drumcree Orangeman, refusing to be rerouted. As a result, he would have to be delivered – in the obstetrical term – 'through the sun-roof'.

On the plus side, this meant I would not have to advise

my wife to push, or to breathe in and out, in that order, and risk mixing it up. But it did mean a visit to the operating theatre, dressed like an extra from *ER*. And it also meant I would have to mind the baby during his mother's recovery period, which took hours.

So there I was on Thursday, pacing the room with my newborn son, who came out hungry and was apparently under the impression that I had bosoms hidden somewhere. Meanwhile, I was starving too.

Protective instinct told me I must not leave the child in any circumstances. It also told me that my car was parked on Merrion Square, the worst place in Dublin for clampers.

So after dashing out twice to feed the meter, I resumed holding the baby, and he resumed sucking my neck, hopefully. At least I could feed the meter, I thought. It was a great relief when the parent the child was looking for finally turned up.

After the baby had docked with its mother ship, I left to fetch the other kids. We went to a café first, where I formally broke the news of the baby's gender, by telling Roisín she was going to be 'even more special' from now on.

It was a corny line, but she fell for it anyway. En route back to Holles Street, we stopped off to buy flowers and an 'It's a boy!' balloon. It was white and blue, of course: just like the Monaghan GAA colours. And then, with Patrick waving the balloon like a team flag, and excitement unbounded, we invaded the hospital.

B Movie: The Tragicomic History of my Leaving Cert English Exams

THE MOST DAZZLING COMPLIMENT I ever received from a schoolteacher was delivered one day in English class, circa 1978, by the late Mr O'Brien.

It seems somewhat less dazzling in retrospect, viewed from an era when high self-esteem comes fitted as standard in teenagers. But all I can say is that it did not then have the slightly sad quality it has acquired in years since.

On the contrary, Mr O'Brien was an ardent admirer of my literary talents. So much so that, when marking essays, he would sometimes hold mine back until last, the better to draw attention to some example of supposed excellence therein, from which the other wretches in our honours English class might benefit.

And sure enough, on this occasion, he went through all their essays first. Then he picked up mine, with an affectionate smile. I have no memory of the topic, or what the thing he liked so much about it was. But having read an extract and allowed my classmates time to savour it – more time than they needed, I'm sure – he proceeded to make a general point about the Leaving Cert exams then looming.

First, he surveyed the room and declared that everyone, with sufficient work, could get honours. There was no one who could not hope for 'at least a Grade C', he added. 'But you,' he said, turning to me, and – I sensed – conferring a sense of responsibility along with the prediction he was about to deliver: '*You* could get a B.'

183

I'm not sure how long after this it first occurred to me that (whisper it) an A should have been considered possible too. It certainly didn't occur then. Yes, even in those days before grade inflation, we must have heard of people getting A's in English.

But if we did, it was probably in Dublin somewhere, by the sort of high-achieving freaks who ended up on the front pages of national newspapers the day after the results came out and who probably paid for their success by not having lives and/or by ending up as actuaries.

Grade A's were the Himalayas of the exam system; in our school, we were training only for the Alps, and had to practise on drumlins. So a grade B was the dizzy summit of my ambition. And I knew it might require oxygen equipment to get even that far. Still, blushing from Mr O'Brien's endorsement, I was determined to try.

Then the exam happened and, if it had been an actual mountain, I would have had to be airlifted off it to safety. I can't recall all the things I did wrong that day, but the least forgivable was not reading the paper properly and omitting a compulsory question. Yes, the one mistake that is drummed into you not to make.

In the essay section, the fiendish examiners had also given us an opportunity to write about our favourite band. For me then, the band was Pink Floyd. Unfortunately, 'favourite' understated the enthusiasm I felt for them. My devotion was more cult-like. And, as I learned that day, sometimes you can know and feel too much about a subject to explain it to sceptical strangers while under time pressure.

Anyway, two months later, I was the owner of a grade D in English: a personal humiliation worsened by the shame of having let down my number one fan, Mr O'Brien.

Oh well. I was still only 16 then. Not having a better plan yet, I repeated the Leaving Cert. This time, I could give up certain subjects and take on new ones. And I could have another go at English, getting that elusive B at the second attempt.

Maybe even grade A was beginning to loom on the horizon. Rumours of such things must have reached me by then, because I had started buying *The Irish Times* every day, where A grades were common currency.

The newspaper habit, considered weird by contemporaries, foreshadowed a vocation in journalism. Writing for a national paper was certainly my ambition, albeit a vague one, because I didn't yet know anyone who did it in real life.

In the meantime, I happily lost myself every day in reading about the world's troubles. Some mornings, you could almost feel the flames of foreign war zones rising from the pages. On one memorable occasion, they turned out to be actual flames, because a mischievous classmate had set fire to the bottom of my paper (if you're reading this, Gerard Martin, you're still a bollocks).

Our English teacher at this point was Mr Flanagan – a nice man, albeit one who refused the right of the final 't' in Samuel Beckett's *Waiting for Godot* to remain silent. I never had the heart to correct him.

He liked my essays too. Yet I could tell there was something about them that worried him. One day after the Mocks, he laid my latest attempt out on the desk and said it was well written, and structured, and all that: 'But it's too short.'

I looked at it, hurt. It was almost two foolscap pages. Whereas, Mr Flanagan explained, now pointing to the example of other classmates as something *I* needed to follow, 'you're expected to write five'. The shortfall would affect my grade unless rectified, he warned.

And God knows I tried. But speaking of Beckett, if there was one thing we had in common, it was a weakness for minimalism. I just couldn't bring myself to write five pages where two seemed to cover a subject adequately.

In my second Leaving Cert English exam, I dragged the essay out to nearly three pages, with what must have been padding and a plethora of unnecessary adjectives. For that and the rest of the paper, I was awarded a grade C.

Sigh. Never mind an A: the B that Mr O'Brien had foreseen would always be beyond me now. In some ways, getting a C at the second attempt was a worse humiliation than the bare pass of a year earlier.

My Leaving Cert results were in general mediocre: a B in History was the nearest I got to excellence. And in defence now, I could claim – somewhat fashionably, these days – to be one of those people to whom the exam format is unsuited.

On the other hand, a few years later, as a very humble and very bored civil servant, I applied for an internal promotion called the 'Adult Ex'. It sounds like a porn movie classification, but the 'Ex' was an abbreviation of Executive Officer and the 'Adult' was to differentiate it from the 'Junior Ex'.

The exam comprised an aptitude test and a series of about 10 English texts you had to reduce to a paragraph or two each. This turned out to be so well suited to my limited skillset that, setting about it, I was like the proverbial dog with two sexual appendages.

A few years later again, as mentioned previously, I became the token mature student on a MA in Journalism course at Dublin City University, which was in some ways similar. All the others in the class had recently completed primary degrees, unlike me. On the plus side, I had a few years' experience of actual freelance journalism.

So now the roles were reversed. My junior classmates had to be deprogrammed: learning to write shorter than they were used to doing, something many of them found difficult. I was already a practised miniaturist.

After that, another few years passed and, by then an established journalist, I was presented with what should have been the ultimate revenge over my bad Leaving Cert English results: being the subject of a question in the 2010 exams.

Strictly speaking, it was only the Mock Leaving Cert English paper. But still. The question centred on a 'colour piece' I had written about Ladies' Day at the Galway Races two years earlier.

And of course I was flattered. Even more so when the question noted that the excerpt was 'adapted' from the original. This made me sound gratifyingly like James Joyce: as if my high-concept metaphors about women's hats had needed simplification for teenage readers.

For the record, the original piece included a riff on the theme of the supposed dangers of being in the marquee where the shortlisted ladies were judged:

The risk involved in having so many pointy hats and parasols – not to mention stilettos – in a confined space was bad enough. But the colours alone could have blinded you. They were of a range and intensity that, to be seen in one place, would normally require the use of psychedelic drugs.

Yellow, amber, tangerine, burnt orange – those

187

were just the fake tans. The clothes were even more vibrant. Searches for this season's new black, or for any predominant theme, were useless. It was like an explosion in a paint factory. The male reporter's stock of colour adjectives – never up to describing Festival Thursday in Ballybrit, even in subdued years – was quickly exhausted.

And all right, they were probably never going to use my reference to 'psychedelic drugs' in a Leaving Cert exam. But unhappily, I discovered, the adaptation of the colour theme consisted chiefly of adding some makey-up comments that I had 'overheard' from spectators at the fashion awards, one of which was: 'My money's on the lady in red!'

Not only had this not happened. But if a spectator really had said something as cheesy as that, and I had quoted it, public horse-whipping in Eyre Square would have been too good for me.

Again, for the record, these were the actual crowd comments quoted in my original:

To judge from the expressions of those watching, the winning outfits evoke a whole gamut of emotions: from admiration to physical pain. Comments in the crowd also range from the generous ('Isn't she lovely?') to the critical ('I wouldn't have picked that'), to the truly damning ('It's certainly different').

Even worse, the adaptation included a misspelling I hadn't made. The original report referred to a famous real-life jockey called Paul Townend. My literary adaptor obviously decided that this couldn't be correct and, without checking, changed it to 'Townsend'.

Thus, my immortalisation on a Leaving Cert English exam paper featured both patently fabricated dialogue and a misspelt surname. After which, the paper cruelly asked students: 'What is your impression of the writer?'

At least I was spared their answers. But of course, the experience only added to the residual trauma of my own Leaving Cert English exams. It was like getting a grade D all over again.

Around the same time, in what could also have been a healing experience, *The Irish Times* asked me and several other ageing reporters to sit a Leaving Cert exam of our choice, for a summer filler series. We would receive the papers after the event, and complete them alone, in empty rooms, a situation that relied on our honesty. But the results would be marked by official examiners, with the same rules and rigour they applied to students.

I was very tempted to try English again and see if I could finally vindicate Mr O'Brien and get that elusive B, or maybe even an A. On the other hand, as someone who by then wrote for a living, full-time, I feared that to subject my efforts to an examiner's grading might be giving hostages to fortune. In the end, I chickened out of doing English. Lest history repeat itself, I played it safe and repeated History.

Driven Round the Bend:
Between a Rock and a Hard Place at Euro 2012
10 June 2016

I THOUGHT THE POST-TRAUMATIC STRESS disorder arising from my experiences at the 2012 European football championships had been fully cured until an email arrived this week and caused flashbacks.

It was from a car rental company about a survey of Irish fans heading to the latest tournament. Among other things, it suggested that half those travelling would hire vehicles of some kind. Then it added, soberingly, that 'one in seven' respondents had reported 'at least one accident or minor "prang" while driving abroad in the past'.

Happily, I did not have any crashes at Euro 2012. I did, however, have something you could call a prang, to which we'll return shortly. But if I suffered any long-term damage, it was from the stress of combining a family holiday with daily dispatches for *The Irish Times* (never again!), while also making my debut as the driver of a rented seven-seater camper van.

The challenges started early when, having secured the last such van in northern Europe, from a company on the Dutch–German border, I had to drive it back into Amsterdam and park overnight. Amsterdam, as you'll have heard, is a bicycle town. And although most of its bikes are of the 'granny' type, they tend to be cycled with an aggression not normally associated with female grandparents, at least in Ireland.

It must be stressful driving even a small smart car

around that city, never mind a large camper, with outsized wing mirrors. Everywhere I went in Amsterdam, I felt as welcome as a Russian tank driver in 1968 Prague. Still, at least the van was unscathed.

There were similar horrors one night in Hanover, where I had to follow complicated directions to a car park just as German fans spilled into the streets to celebrate a win. The van's blind spots were big enough already without flags draped over the windscreen. But due to this and other distractions, I drove the wrong way up a one-way street, full of drunks, while police – perhaps noticing the cold sweat – waved me on.

There too, the vehicle went undamaged. And more remarkably, it also survived all of Poland, although there are roads in that country where two sets of outsized wing mirrors were not meant to meet.

Seeing a lorry approach, often, I would hug the kerb and hope for the best. But hug as I might, the experience of seeing trucks speed past in the opposite direction gave me an insight into what it must have felt like being a medieval knight in a jousting tournament.

Sure enough, among other camper drivers I met in Poland were a group of Irish lads who had lost a wing-mirror in action. Their plan was to replace it locally and hope the hire company wouldn't see the join.

That option was not available to me, alas, when the rental van and I finally ran out of luck. It happened in a suburban *sackgasse* (cul-de-sac) in Magdeburg, on one of the many occasions we got lost trying to find a campsite.

By the time I realised it was a *sackgasse*, it was too late. Reversing back out in a vehicle with a blind spot the width of the vehicle, past a row of parked BMWs, was unthinkable.

But as if to repel just such vehicles as ours, the already small turning area at the end of the *sackgasse* was guarded by a giant boulder, disguised under greenery (and darkness). I only noticed the boulder when, during the early stages of a 52-point turn, I heard an ominous crack somewhere.

This proved to be the van's protective side panel, between the wheels. And when I later surveyed the damage in daylight, it seemed like a cruel joke on the whole Irish-football-fan experience. Yes, the crack was 90 (centimetres), give or take.

That was bad enough. So was the challenge of extricating myself without making things worse. But as I walked around the vehicle, surveying the situation, what made it even more grim was the realisation that I was stuck in the middle a cliché.

On one side, severely limiting my options, was the boulder. On the other side was a fence surrounding the *sackgasse*'s end. It was only a wooden fence. Yet it was nonetheless immovable. There could be no denying it: I was caught between a rock and a hard place.

The operation that followed was among the most fraught driving experiences of my life. Aside from the fact that, whichever way I turned, there seemed to be only centimetres of leeway, there was the added problem that, from the driver's seat, I couldn't see the rock.

So I had to do what mariners have always done with rocks – put a lighthouse on it. Or in this case my 12-year-old son, Patrick. He stood on the middle of the boulder, with orders to shout if the van's headlights got too near the shoreline underneath. His mother, meanwhile, manned the fence.

In this manner, to the percussive accompaniment of 'Rock!', 'Fence!', 'Rock!' – and with a few similarly

Anglo-Saxon-sounding expressions from myself thrown in – I eventually waltzed the juggernaut around until, after only 10 minutes or so, it was facing out of the road again.

Driving away, I sensed that the van and I had both been scarred by the experience. But at least they could fix the van. If I never see a *sackgasse* again, it'll still be too soon.

Having forgotten to take out excess-damage insurance, I briefly considered a 500-mile side trip to Turin, to get a replica panel from Fiat. That would probably have been cheaper.

In the end, I had to surrender to the mercies of the German camper-van hire people, who were not feeling merciful. While I awaited their mechanic's verdict, the office woman regaled me with the various misfortunes of the fleet returning from Poland. She sounded as mournful as the queen of Spain discussing the fate of the Armada. And I knew this was just softening me up for the impending blow.

But in search of consolation, I asked what the most expensive prang had been. That's when she mentioned the camper driver who had managed to write off a 'brand-new Audi' somewhere. Ouch. Continuing to await the mechanic's return, I consoled myself that, so long as it is a low-speed collision, there are worse things to hit than a boulder.

Voices from the Grave: A Tale of Two Long-lost Ancestors

AT THE RISK OF ROMANTICISING him – and some terms and conditions *do* apply – my namesake grandfather, Frank McNally Sr, was a lawman in the American Wild West.

I never got to ask him about his adventures there because we never met. He died, aged 87, before I was born. His exploits on the frontier are unrecorded anywhere I can find. And they might have escaped me completely had I not extracted a very brief account of them once from his only son, my father.

The latter is now long gone too. But in his later years, when we belatedly took to having the occasional conversation – still an optional extra then in relationships between Irish fathers and sons – I once asked in passing what his old man had done in America, during the years I knew he spent there, circa 1900.

That's when I first learned, between puffs of my father's pipe, that Frank McNally Sr had been a 'deputy sheriff in Montana'. This news was delivered as if having been a deputy sheriff in Montana was only slightly more interesting than being, say, inspector of drains for Longford (à la Percy French).

But my imagination ran riot at the thought. Suddenly I had visions of Granddad McNally riding with posses across badlands, or facing down dangerous outlaws in saloons while other customers ducked for cover, or perhaps getting involved in the odd shoot-out at a corral, OK or otherwise.

Further details were not to be had from my father,

however. And years later, when I visited Butte – the once-famous copper mining city to which my grandfather and two of his sisters had travelled in the 1890s – the trail was just as hard to pick up there.

Thanks to a street census of 1897, I did eventually track down the right names (Francis, Annie and Mary McNally), at least, in a lodging house in nearby Anaconda. That was the smelting town built and named after the all-powerful mining company, which was in turn named after the giant snake that smothers and eats its prey – even some large animals – whole. They didn't do subtlety in Montana.

Alas, my hopes that the local police department would provide clinching information were dashed. The sheriffs for Deer Lodge County, in which Anaconda sits, are indeed all listed in the archives. They had to run for election. But their mere deputies, presumably added to the ticket afterwards, remain anonymous. The best the police could do was give me one of those sew-on badges from the sheriff's department, an honorary recognition of my ancestral claims.

The museum in Anaconda was unable to help either. But the curator sensed my need for romantic detail, however vague, and duly obliged. 'Those were dangerous times in these parts,' he said. 'A lot of deputy sheriffs got shot.' I was thrilled to hear it.

Having established that, at least in theory, my ancestral namesake could have been a hero, like Pat Garrett or Wyatt Earp, I should now confess that my use of the terms 'Wild West' and 'frontier' earlier were stretching it slightly. Born in 1870, Granddad McNally would have been only six years old when, in another corner of Montana, General Custer met his end at the hands of Crazy Horse and Sitting Bull.

Thereafter, despite that rare win for the Native Americans, the days of the untamed west were numbered. Fourteen years later, in 1890, the frontier – the boundary between the settled and unsettled parts of the US – was declared closed.

So the west was no longer officially wild when my grandfather got there. Which said, Butte in its heyday – just beginning then – may have given 'wild' a whole new layer of meaning.

All those miners needed places to spend their money. Many bars opened 24 hours a day. And among other claims to infamy, Butte is said to have once had America's second-largest red light district, after only New Orleans.

Whatever he did in Montana, my grandfather returned to Ireland, eventually, in time to be listed in the 1911 census. He got married sometime between then and 1913 and again a few years later – to my father's mother this time – after his first wife died giving birth to my Auntie Rois.

His tracks next turn up in newspapers during the revolutionary period, by which time he was a local politician. He became a Sinn Féin councillor in 1920 and a magistrate in the short-lived Republican courts. He opposed the 1921 Treaty, then lost his seat in 1925 when Monaghan heavily backed the Treaty, or, as *The Northern Standard* put it, 'turned against the wild men'.

Thereafter, my grandfather disappears back into private life and fragmentary anecdote, handed down by friends and neighbours. I'm told he was a founding member of Fianna Fáil in 1926, running the Mile River Cumann, north of Carrickmacross, from a disused railway carriage beside his house. He wore hobnailed boots with no socks, even in winter. He once fired a shotgun at a 'tramp' found trespassing on his property.

He was an early riser and went early to bed. Even if he had visitors, he retired religiously every night at 9pm, dropping hints to any stragglers by standing up at that time, stretching, and winding the clock.

Getting back to his public days circa 1920, whenever quoted in the local newspapers (mainly during a period he spent on the Poor Law Union committee, which oversaw the old 'workhouses' that predated the county homes), he comes across as financially conservative, to say the least. Like many at that time, he probably thought that people in workhouses were there through their own fault – for drinking too much, typically – and that their bad choices should not be subsidised by hard-pressed rate-payers.

And those were hard times in Ireland. At one meeting, when the question of payment for doctors' visits to inmates came up, my grandfather couldn't understand why their rates were still the same as in previous years. It was an era of general economic depression, he pointed out. If the price farmers' wives got for eggs was falling, why shouldn't doctors be paid less too?

That was fair enough, I suppose. But he was sceptical of social spending in general, to an extent that, reading it as a bleeding-heart liberal from the comfort of the twenty-first century, I sometimes squirmed.

I know one shouldn't need to apologise for dead ances-tors: it's not as if we have any influence over them, unlike our children. Even so, poring over old newspapers, I was regularly embarrassed by my grandfather's hard-line fiscal austerity. 'Shut up about the bloody rate-payers,' I found myself telling him on occasion.

His reputation earned the dubious tribute once of a verse by John McEnaney, aka 'The Bard of Callenberg'.

Callenberg was a townland near Inniskeen, and long before Patrick Kavanagh immortalised the general area, McEnaney was locally famous as a satirist. He was also famous for being a drunk, and for giving bards a bad name, something Kavanagh recalled when describing his parents' fears about his own early drift towards poetry.

Sure enough, McEnaney had spent time in the workhouse. From where, protesting my grandfather's perennial defence of the rate-payers, he once sent a satirical lament to the Poor Law committee. Unfortunately, I can't quote it. Having found it in a library search years ago, I haven't been able to relocate it, or the note I took, since.

There was another notorious occasion, during the changeover from workhouses to county homes, when the subject of an inmate being discharged for Christmas came up for debate at a Poor Law committee meeting. Having no other transport, apparently, the man had been forced to walk the almost 30 miles from Monaghan town to Carrickmacross, in the depths of winter.

And almost everyone on the committee thought this was a disgrace. They took turns to express outrage at the medical negligence involved and demanded those responsible be summoned to explain themselves at the next meeting. All except my grandfather. Typically, he wondered why the home – and by extension the inevitable rate-payers – were expected to provide a free taxi service.

In the National Library reading room nearly a century later, I was mortified anew. Then I turned to the next week's paper, with trepidation. Wherein – lo! – it turned out that at the follow-up meeting, both the county home and my grandfather had been vindicated.

It was the management's turn to be outraged by their misrepresentation a week earlier, as it emerged that the inmate had checked himself out on Christmas Eve, against medical advice, and was allowed to leave only after assuring staff he had a lift arranged. The Poor Law guardians were forced to dismount from their high horses and apologise. Only the ex-deputy sheriff from Montana emerged blameless.

My grandfather had returned from the US after earning enough money to buy some land back in Ireland. This was typical of Irish emigrants. Men came home if they could. Women, having few prospects here, stayed and embraced their American freedoms.

His sisters Annie and Mary spent the rest of their lives in Montana. And by contrast with him, they left behind impeccable records of their time there, ranging from their own gravestones to living descendants. It is also to them that I owe the only piece of (literally) hard evidence about my grandfather's lawmaking career.

When I visited my cousin Rosie, a school principal in Butte, in 2004, she gave it to me as a present, having inherited it from her grandmother, who had in return received it from her brother, Frank McNally Sr, maybe 100 years earlier. It was a 'night stick': a short, heavy, lead-filled truncheon, left behind as a memento when, with the west successfully subdued, my granddad returned home to Monaghan.

No, it wasn't quite the Colt revolver I would have hoped for, with a notch on the barrel for every no-good outlaw who had crossed his path. The night stick suggested a city beat rather than the Badlands. Well-worn though it was, it represented the march of progress, as the former frontier became urbanised.

Still, I was delighted to receive it. DNA and my name aside, it's the only souvenir I have of Frank McNally Sr.

Who, by the time I was born, was just a behatted and moustachioed stranger staring out at us from an old sepia-tinted picture on the wall.

He looks just as stern as he sounded in those newspaper quotes. I search in vain for the hint of a twinkle in his eye. And I'm not sure he would have appreciated the joke of an *Irish Times* letter writer who, after I mentioned my grandfather's journey from Monaghan to Montana and back, wondered if he was the 'first recorded cowboy in Fianna Fáil'.

***

Losing the memory of one interesting ancestor might have been considered unfortunate, to paraphrase Oscar Wilde. Two would have seemed like carelessness.

And yet somehow I managed to reach advanced middle age before first hearing of a relative who was widely known in his lifetime as the 'last of the great Irish harpers'. Worse, in this case, I didn't find out about him by asking questions myself. I only learned the story by accident, thanks to the curiosity of others.

One day in 2009, the Carrickmacross branch of Comhaltas Ceoltóirí Éireann emailed me at *The Irish Times* asking for a mention of their new annual festival, held in honour of a local musician called Blind Patrick Byrne. A celebrity in his lifetime, they said, he had played all over Britain and Ireland, his many admirers including British royalty. Among other distinctions, he was the first Irish traditional musician ever photographed.

But somewhat mysteriously, after his death in 1863, he had ended up buried in the paupers' cemetery in Carrick, aka Bully's Acre. Then he lapsed into obscurity for the next 150 years. Now, at last, his memory was being reclaimed.

My first reaction on hearing the story was to marvel not just that such a man had once existed in my hometown but that the town – which is hardly overwhelmed with famous dead – had managed to forget him. I regarded this as collective negligence on the community's part. Or was it wilful neglect? The suspicion arose because Byrne's tombstone mentioned that he had been harper 'by royal appointment' to Prince Albert (husband of Queen Victoria).

Had he been deliberately expunged from local memory for being, in a Republican part of Ireland, politically incorrect? Either way, I felt somewhat indignant at the town's amnesia about a once-famous son. That was before I realised he was my great-great-grand-uncle.

But first to what Comhaltas were able to tell me in 2009. This included the facts that Byrne was born in about 1794, in the southwest corner of Monaghan, at Magheracloone, to a poor, Catholic, and Irish-speaking family.

The blindness came soon afterwards, the result of smallpox when he was two, and probably marked him for a career in music. Details of his early life were scarce, unfortunately. But by age 17, when the Earl of Moira arranged for him to be sent to an institution, where he first learned to speak English, Byrne was going up in the world.

There had been around the time of his birth a politically inspired revival of interest in Ireland's ancient cultural traditions. Of special interest were the old-style harpers, a threatened species when music collector Edward Bunting gathered the known survivors for a festival in Belfast in 1792. Among the 10 veterans who turned up, six were blind. One was 97, another 80 and a third in his 70s.

The United Irishmen were enthusiastic supporters: some more than others. Wolfe Tone had mixed feelings. After the first Belfast performance, he noted in his diary that three of the performers were good, but seven 'execrable'. By the third night, he was losing patience: 'The harpers again,' he muttered. 'Strum, strum, and be hanged.'

But 30 years later, as the blood-soaked 1798 rebellion faded from memory, the Belfast Harp Society was founded in another attempt to revive the music. It was here that Pádraig Dall Ó Beirn – as he was still known then – came in. He studied the instrument in Belfast, where he was later presented with a special harp in recognition of his diligence, his 'good deportment as a scholar' and his proficiency in '60 tunes'.

He was now championed by his Monaghan landlords, the Shirleys, through whose influence the doors of Irish and English high society were opened to him, including the queen's. Byrne was important enough to feature in a milestone event in the then embryonic science of photography. That was circa 1845, at a costumed ball in Edinburgh. The picture shows him in other-worldly garb, worn for the part of the elderly musician from Walter Scott's epic poem *The Lay of the Last Minstrel*.

His harp was wire-strung, as Irish harps had been for centuries, and he was plucking it with his fingernails in the old style – a style that, if it wasn't dead already, would die with him. (In that and other pictures, he looks the image of one of my Magheracloone uncles, Frank Murray.)

While the style in general is now extinct, we have been left a strong flavour of Byrne's playing in the description by a writer who remembered his performances of 'Brian Boru's March', complete with the harper's own running commentary:

After quaffing a generous tumbler of punch, he would say: 'Now, ladies and gentlemen, I am going to play you the celebrated march of the great King Brian to the head of Clontarf, when he gave the Danes such a drubbing. The Irish army is far off, but if you listen attentively you will hear the faint sound of their music.'

Then his fingers would wander over the upper range of strings with so delicate a touch that you might fancy it was fairy music heard from a distance. Anything more fine, more soft and delicate than this performance, it is impossible to conceive. 'They are coming nearer!' [he would say]. And the sound increased in volume. 'Now here they are!' And the music rolled loud and full.

Thus the march went on; the fingers of the minstrel's right hand wandering farther down the bass range ... Then the music became stronger and louder, [including] a deeper rumbling of the bass, with an occasional harmonic third with the right hand, producing a remarkable effect. 'Now they're at it – Irish and Danes!'

The music suddenly changes to the middle range; it is hard and harsh – Clang! Clang! Like the fall of sword or axe on armour, the blows showering thickly; and that harmonic third aforesaid comes frequently, but on a higher string, which gives it a sterner and more fitting effect.

And so the old harper's performance would continue, until the Irish won the battle. Then:

Immediately the music assumes a merry, lightsome character, as if it were played for dancers ... But this abruptly ceases; there is another shriek and discord, jangling and confusion in the upper bass strings. The harper explains as usual: 'They have found the old King murdered in his tent.'

In keeping with the aristocratic traditions of harping, Byrne played few public concerts, even at the height of his career. Instead, he gave private paid recitals in the homes of the gentry, staying with them for periods, then travelling on.

An exception was in 1856 in Scotland, when pick-pockets relieved him of £14 10s, the savings of a summer, which he was carrying, according to a local news report, 'with the characteristic heedlessness of an Irishman'. Friends suggested that, to compensate, he should give a public performance. A capacity attendance subsequently paid to hear his repertoire of old airs, songs, jokes and stories, and was enraptured. 'That a poor blind man should have sustained close attention and interest for nearly two hours is indeed something remarkable,' wrote the *Belfast Newsletter.*

There had been more than one 'last of the great Irish harpers', it must be said. Byrne was part of a tradition stretching back a thousand years and more. But it had been dying for centuries, a process speeded up by Elizabeth I when, after the Battle of Kinsale, she ordered her military to 'hang the harpers [and] burn their instruments'. That the great Turlough O'Carolan flourished more than 100 years later suggests the queen's orders were less than completely successful.

Even so, during Byrne's lifetime he was routinely described as the man with whom the saga would end. As music historian Keith Sanger has written: 'Patrick Byrne certainly was the last of the line of harpers whose traditional status came from playing to the top of the social tree.'

He appears to have been reconciled to this role. He had no pupil to bequeath his harp to, asking instead that the Shirleys should display it for future generations. On an 1855 homecoming to Carrickmacross, he was presented with a 'purse of gold' in recognition of his life's achievements.

After that, he survived long enough to merit mention in a then-new Dublin newspaper, *The Irish Times*, which in 1860 called him 'a venerable relic of a bygone age' and 'the last and best representative of Ireland's ancient harp music'. When he died at Dundalk in 1863, he was at first buried there. Then, in keeping with directions in his will, he was reinterred in his hometown.

***

All this I wrote about while plugging the 2009 Feile Patrick Byrne. Then a year passed, and another festival loomed.

In the meantime, Comhaltas had been digging through various archives. Now, in what at first looked like an ingenious PR strategy to secure a repeat mention in the paper, they emailed again with the news: 'We think this man's related to you.'

The facts by then established were these. Byrne, who never wed, had no known children. And although his father's three marriages produced several half-siblings – including a brother Christopher, who fought in the US Civil War – the harper himself had only one full sibling: a sister who was called 'Alice the beautiful'.

Alice married a man named Ward and together they

had a son, James, the main lineal descendant, to whom the harper bequeathed his 'watch, seals, and other watch appendages'. That James Ward in turn had four children, including one named Annie. And, as I now realised, thanks to Comhaltas, I knew the Annie Ward in question. As a child, in fact, I had visited her on her deathbed, because she was my maternal grandmother.

This appeared to make me a descendant of the last of the great Irish harpers: a crippling responsibility to inherit suddenly in your mid-40s. As I wrote while plugging the 2010 Feile: 'I wonder if it's too late to start classes?'

But the revelation also made the mystery of his burial place and subsequent obscurity a matter of personal interest. Why had I never heard about this man – easily the most famous ancestor in the family tree – until now? And how had he ended up in the paupers' cemetery?

The mystery deepened because he was in anything but a pauper's grave. On the contrary, in a place almost devoid of recognisable gravestones, Byrne's is a stately 'table tomb', proclaiming his royal patronage (a detail some visitor over the years has tried to censor with a chisel).

It was said in various accounts of his life that he had at some point converted to the Church of Ireland, and that in his will he asked to be buried in Carrick's 'new Protestant cemetery'. But what became the new cemetery, named in the Moravian style as 'God's Acre', opened only in the 1890s, too late for him. And if the nearby Bully's Acre had temporarily served as a Protestant burial ground, as some scholars think, Byrne's headstone there is a conspicuously lonely one.

On the other hand, even his supposed religious conversion seemed a mystery. The only written evidence is his will, and newspaper reports from the 1840s mentioning his membership of two masonic lodges in Scotland.

That was after the papal ban of 1826, when even Daniel O'Connell had to give up his freemasonry habit. And we know that the landlord, Evelyn P. Shirley, took great trouble to give Byrne a Protestant burial, his agent having warned that the 'papist relatives' might want to take the body elsewhere.

But in a talk given at the 2013 Feile, the local Church of Ireland rector, Robert Kingston, was sceptical about whether Byrne ever converted. The masonic ban meant little then, he argued, the pope having had to reiterate it many times afterwards.

As for the will, that bore 'the hand of Shirley', thought Kingston. Furthermore, Byrne's tombstone inscription 'requiescat in pace', being a prayer for the dead, was a mainly Catholic thing. And whatever about dying Protestant, Kingston added, Byrne was not buried as one. There is no mention of the event in the Church of Ireland 'burial book'.

Since first hearing of the family connection, I wondered if the seeming silence that followed the harper's death arose from embarrassment at an ancestor who had 'taken the soup', as the damning phrase puts it. Now I wonder if his burial in a paupers' graveyard was not some sort of compromise between a proselytising landlord and 'papist' relatives ready to reclaim him for a faith they thought he never left.

We know that one of the things he had done with his musical wealth was erect a handsome headstone to his father in the Catholic churchyard at Magheracloone. That has a certain Protestant quality, praising Thomas Byrne (d. 1843) 'as a hard working, honest industrious man and a kind good-hearted neighbour'. But it's undeniably affectionate and also boasts of the family's deep roots in an area where it had lived 'for upwards of 200 years'.

Patrick Byrne may have been an accidental Protestant for much of his adult life. As he travelled from one Big House family to another in Ireland and Britain, politeness to his hosts must have played a part in where he went to church on Sundays. There may not have been much choice at times. Blind from infancy and without any other means to make a living, he had always depended on the kindness of strangers.

It's poignant that, despite his fame and many powerful friends, the great musician reposes in a cemetery for the poorest of the poor. But this hardly matters to him now, anyway. When I stood at the grave on his April anniversary a while back, the hillside around us awash with sunshine and primroses, it seemed as good a place as any to end up.

Bonaparte at the Seams: Napoleonic Wars Revisited, with my Friend Steve

I KNEW STEVE DUNFORD FOR only about five years, but it felt more like 25. We first met at the French ambassador to Ireland's Bastille Day party in 2016, where Steve was one of a group of eccentrics dressed in military costume from the Napoleonic era.

Having 12 months earlier witnessed a bicentennial re-enactment of the Battle of Waterloo, with more than 6,000 such enthusiasts from all over Europe, I was fascinated to meet local members of this strange cult. And sure enough, it turned out that 'General Dunford', as he was known to friends and admirers, had also been part of the 2015 Waterloo spectacular.

But while we chatted about that, he presented me with a silver lapel pin in the shape of a pike, commemorating the insurrection of 1798, Ireland's 'Year of the French'. This was a fateful moment.

Although I didn't realise it then, I had just been recruited into his army reserve (as a mere 'Private McNally', a station above which I was never to rise). I would see him present many of those pins in the years after.

Your mother never warns you about the dangers of taking lapel pins from strangers, so I accepted mine in all innocence. Then one thing led to another. And two years to the day later, still wearing the pin, I found myself in France, in the hometown of 1798 hero General Jean Joseph Amable Humbert, being handed an eighteenth-century uniform and a gun, and invited to join the army.

Compared with Steve and the other re-enactors of military history who had assembled there, I was getting off lightly. They buy their own costumes (my habit of calling them that used to draw regular corrections from Steve: 'They're uniforms, Frank!') and weapons, at great expense. They are also martyrs to airport security, not to mention baggage charges.

My ensemble, by contrast, was on loan from one of the French volunteers, and waiting for me at the hotel. But getting off lightly did not extend to wearing the damn thing.

It was 30-something degrees in France that day, so when I was first handed the uniform, my heart sank. The rest of me sank when I put it on, starting with the knee-length shirt and breeches, then the sash, waistcoat, tunic, cravat and after that the cross-belt with sword and bayonet, and the other belt with ammunition box, plus of course the bread-bag, also worn over the shoulder.

With my bicorne hat in place, I thought I was fully kitted. But no. An inspection by Michel, the uniform owner whose fiercely expressive body language made up for his lack of English, produced consternation. I had forgotten my spats – *quelle horreur!* – which he had to fish out of one of the bags and button onto my shoes himself.

An intensive five-minute training course later, Steve deemed me ready to be hidden somewhere in the second rank for the day's manoeuvres. It was not a battle re-enactment: those can be genuinely dangerous and a neophyte like me wouldn't be allowed near them.

I had already learned that at the 2015 re-enactment, from the Duke of Wellington himself. Or at least from Alan Larsen, the New Zealand-born actor who made part of his living from playing the Duke in such events, and whom I interviewed at the post-battle press conference.

Blank though the ammunition used in re-enactments is, it can be fatal in the wrong hands, as Larsen told me. Back in 1986, as a young man, he was almost killed at an event in England. A rifleman who fired at him had inadvertently left the brass tip of a ramrod in the muzzle, effectively adding a bullet to the gunpowder (which on its own just produces a flash and bang).

It sliced through Larsen's carotid artery and, when he fell forwards, those around him thought he was playing dead. Only when he was turned over minutes later, and a geyser of blood shot up, did he receive attention. Had there not been an ex-army doctor nearby, he would not have survived to play the duke.

I didn't hear of any real bullets at the 2015 Waterloo. But as the pretend fighting began, and the fields in front of us gradually filled with smoke, real twenty-first-century stretcher bearers were soon emerging from it, carrying the genuinely injured away, from gunpowder burns, horse-falls and other accidents.

On Bastille Day 2018, we were mostly just marching and standing to attention as part of Remiremont's annual celebrations, which also include the real, modern French army and emergency services. Nevertheless, I still sweat at the memory of it.

They didn't know much in Remiremont about what we call the Year of the French. And what they did know was thanks to the likes of Steve, whose enthusiasm for the subject dated back at least to his teenage years, when he was in a band called General Humbert (whose members included a certain Mary Black).

So it being the 220th anniversary of '98, we also marked

that Bastille weekend with an even sweatier march the following morning, Sunday, through the foothills of the Vosges mountains to General Humbert's ancestral farm.

There we fired volleys in Humbert's honour, and when our hosts sang 'La Marseillaise', we responded with an impromptu 'Amhrán na bhFiann'. I can't vouch for the quality of our unrehearsed singing and wouldn't want to hear a recording. Even so – and perhaps influenced by the wine that was being served generously – the locals declared themselves moved by the performance.

Then General Dunford press-ganged me into joining him on a diplomatic side mission to Plombières-les-bains, a once famous spa town where, in 1858, Napoleon III and Count Cavour negotiated a treaty while circling the streets in a carriage.

We circled the streets too, driven by the mayor (in a car this time, although the town's layout can't have changed much since 1858; some of the alleyways were so narrow our driver had to reach out and close window shutters to let us pass).

The mayor then treated us to dinner, after which he brought us to the local cinema, where the World Cup final – in which France beat Croatia – was being screened live.

By the time we got back to Remiremont, thirsty, after a long, hot day promoting Mayo and Ireland (Steve's unofficial and unpaid job), we looked forward to celebrating the French victory late into the night.

Imagine our chagrin when, instead, the local bourgeoisie went to bed early, as usual, and the last pubs closed at 10pm. This was France, not Ireland. World Cup or no World Cup, people were planning to get up in time for work next morning.

Still in uniform, Steve and I were walking the now

deserted streets in forlorn hope of finding a private house party somewhere when we met a group of Vosgiennes getting into a car, carrying take-away pints. They were first astonished by the sight of two bedraggled Napoleonic soldiers, then doubly surprised to learn we were Irish. No, they'd never heard of General Humbert either, of course.

But a five-minute history lesson later, General Dunford was presenting them with silver pike pins from his apparently inexhaustible supply. The charmed recipients were initially at a loss as to how to reciprocate such generosity.

Then Steve dropped a hint about how disappointing it was that the pubs had closed so early. Whereupon his latest army recruits happily donated their beers. Thus it was that we liberated the last two pints in Remiremont on World Cup night.

I was lucky, by the way, not to be court-martialled that weekend. During a lunchtime reception at the mayoralty, and needing two hands for the wine glass and canapés, I leaned my rifle against a wall nearby. Then we all adjourned to the garden and I forgot about it. When an abandoned rifle was reported to my commanding officer, General D, he was forced to give me a telling off.

It didn't come naturally to him, but he was convincingly stern nonetheless. The expense apart, even period rifles are too dangerous to be allowed go missing at such events. I suspect the carelessness cost any chances of me ever being promoted from private. That and my continuing tendency to use the word 'costume'. ('It's a uniform, Frank!')

Anyway, a year and a bit later, in very different weather, I met Steve again in the Mayo village of Lahardane, which was not the most auspicious place to start a journey. It is now and forever associated with a group of young emigrants who in 1912 left from there to board the *Titanic*. Eleven died in the disaster, and Lahardane today commemorates them with a sculpture garden, among other tributes.

But the village was also on the route of one of the most famous military marches in Irish history, when General Humbert led a small Franco-Irish army south through it from Killala in 1798 to the event that became known as 'the Races of Castlebar'.

Having missed the first two days of a re-enactment that weekend, I strapped myself into uniform (one from Steve's collection this time – he had about half a dozen) just in time to join the last leg of the journey on Sunday morning.

The original trek was overnight, on a trail through bog and mountain, deliberately chosen to wrongfoot English troops in Castlebar, who were defending the main road.

So apart from us having had a night's sleep, and breakfast, beforehand, our 'In Humbert's Footsteps' march was to be authentically that: skirting a clouded-over Nephin mountain and braving the 'Windy Gap' before descending on Mayo's county town, 23km away, via the original route.

The weather added realism. It was foul on the night in question in 1798. And although our group left Lahardane in pleasant conditions, by the time we reached the Gap, rain had arrived from nowhere – travelling sideways, as is traditional here – and insisted on accompanying us for the rest of the trip.

It was soft rain, at least. In other circumstances it might even have seemed poetic. But when you're wearing heavy woollen coats and waistcoats and are already weighed down by swords, guns, ammunition boxes and other accoutrements, rain does rather add to the hardship.

Even when dry on the outside, 1790s military costume ('Uniform, Frank!') offers certain internal challenges. The combination of tight knee breeches, strapped-on thigh-high boots, and several belts can be a bit like the stuff they sell in certain adult shops.

But the effects of bondage aside, I had been warned by the general that chafing could be a big problem too. Hence the most intimate part of my outfit that day: a pair of leggings borrowed from Steve's wife, Bernie. You do some terrible things in war.

As for the rain, our logistics department (whose name was Sharon Horkan) turned out to have several plastic raincoats in her bag, along with a range of pain-relief products that would have done honour to a pharmacy.

At the price of some historic credibility, we avoided the uniforms getting wet from the outside in, albeit by increasing the rate at which they were getting wet from the inside out. An army marches in its own sweat, as Napoleon didn't say. And another noteworthy fact about period uniforms – which cost €1,000 upwards – is that you can't really launder them.

They shrink and run too easily, so you can only air them between use. Aired or not, they mature like fine wines, with bouquets to match. Even if mine dried out eventually, I pitied the next person who had to wear it.

Anyway, after five hours of sweaty tramping that Sunday, we made it into Castlebar in one piece, although by then the soles of my feet felt like they'd been beaten by pikestaffs. Afterwards I developed aches in muscles I didn't know I had.

On the plus side, nobody fired cannonballs at us, unlike the original marchers, who suffered heavy early casualties before overrunning the English and forcing a rapid retreat. That was where the 'Races of Castlebar' gibe arose. In our case, we had to make do with overrunning a local food fair, slaughtering several innocent pints of beer that got in the way.

I say 'pints', but in McHale's Bar later, Steve introduced me to a curious Castlebar phenomenon called the 'Medium', pronounced 'meejum': a time-honoured practice whereby you can order a pint-glass of stout, not quite full.

At first, I assumed this was to leave room for something else to be poured in. But no. The 7/8th measure was a thing in itself: a vestige of poorer times when it allowed a man to seem to have a full pint before him (half-pints being only for ladies then), while saving crucial pennies.

It was a good drink with which to toast General Humbert, who, had he won a few more battles, might have converted Ireland to the metric system a lot sooner. A British imperial pint glass holds 568ml. Filled to 7/8ths, like the Castlebar 'Medium', it's a demi-litre, or near enough.

The other thing Steve got me into in those years was fishing. We spent several pleasant, uniform-free days on a small trawler off Killala, where he lived near the pier, fishing for ling and pollock and mackerel. We would go out in the morning, before the tide did, and return with it seven or eight hours later. In between, we usually caught enough to fill everyone's freezer for weeks afterwards.

Not the least memorable thing about the experience was watching Steve and his brother John (a veteran sound engineer who also happened to be Sharon Shannon's manager) gutting the day's haul on the way back to port. It was some of the most intense work I'd ever seen two men do. But all the fish would be gutted, cleaned and in buckets, with the deck of the boat hosed down, by the time we neared port, followed by a flock of happy seagulls enjoying their evening tea.

This was an apt pastime for the Dunford brothers, who, decades earlier, had both been involved in the making of the Waterboys' classic album *Fisherman's Blues*. That earned Steve a small piece of immortality. He happened to be at a party in Spiddal in 1988 when the band improvised a tune that he recorded on cassette. It ended up on the record as 'Dunford's Fancy'.

The tune is short and sweet, a bit like life itself, as I now think every time I listen to it. Our last outing off Killala and Downpatrick Head must have been in the summer or autumn of 2019, pre-Covid. Little did any of us know then that I would attend both Dunford brothers' funerals before we would ever go fishing again. First Steve, then John, died of lung cancer. John had recently bought the boat they used to hire.

When I last met Steve, in the Mayo Hospice at Castlebar in the autumn of 2021, he was out of uniform but in the wars for real. Still, he was in good spirits, surrounded by his loving family, Bernie, John and Romy, and as usual we ended up laughing, despite the circumstances.

Speaking of the Races of Castlebar, I nearly missed the last train back to Dublin that day because we had so much to talk about, having to run the mile or more to the station with a heavy backpack now further weighed down by the latest of the books Steve was always writing, a history of Killala.

I promised a longer visit soon and meant it, not realising how little time there was left. Hearing a week later that he had left us, I'm not ashamed to say I cried.

Then I remembered his book, still in the bag, and belatedly read the dedication to 'Private McNally'. Even as I promised to visit him again, he had been writing in the past tense. 'Thanks for all the madness – it was a blast,' his inscription read. Then he signed off: 'Your friend Steve Dunford (formerly General).'

Happy as Larry: Finding and Losing an Old Friend in the Covid Pandemic

DURING THE FIRST COVID LOCKDOWN in 2020, a social worker in Monaghan asked me to contribute to a package of reading material she was putting together for local 'cocooners'.

So I chose a few suitable columns and sent them on, doubtful they would be read. And I was astonished and gratified when, months later, they resulted in a letter from a long-lost schoolmate, Lawrence Keenan.

I hadn't heard from Lawrence for nearly 40 years. Whenever I thought of him, as I did from time to time, I wondered if he was still alive. Now suddenly, here he was again, albeit writing to me from a nursing home.

It was a charmingly eccentric letter, begun on one of those free cards An Post issued to care homes, written on both sides, then escalating onto a sheet of paper, and finished off with postscripts around the edges. The address, care of *The Irish Times*, was a short story too, compiled from scraps of known or assumed information and covering much of the envelope.

Somehow it had found me. And I was so delighted to hear from him that I wrote back by return post, promising a visit as soon as possible.

Lawrence came from over near Cullaville, a village on the Monaghan–Armagh border, on the road to Crossmaglen. He attended primary school there and only for secondary did he join us at the Patrician Brothers in Carrickmacross.

I never found out what his family circumstances were,

exactly, except that he was an only child. There were competing theories but nobody knew. Anyway, somehow you sensed he needed minding. And insofar as the rough and tumble of a boys' school allowed, minded he generally was.

He stood out in first year partly because he was taller than most of us – and he should have been, because, as I found out only in 2020, he had been by far the oldest in class back then, at 14 (I was second youngest, at 11).

But height aside, he was also conspicuous for his big red face, accentuated cruelly by a classic 'bowl' haircut. That might pass for fashion now. Back then, it looked like an affliction.

The other extraordinary thing about him was that he had been fitted for school with a three-piece suit – a family heirloom, probably. Nobody else among us wore a suit, not even the teachers. And yet he was still wearing his five years later, when he left.

He had long outgrown it by then, but not as much as he should have. Having started out tall, he seemed to shrink gradually and had a pronounced stoop by the end.

Two small but telling vignettes stayed with me from those years. The first of these came when, one day, a stand-in teacher – a Patrician Brother probably back from the 'foreign missions' – asked everyone in class to state his father's name and occupation. I don't know what the brother was thinking in this – he probably wasn't thinking at all. Nobody would ask that question today, of course.

But when it was Lawrence's turn to answer, we noticed that the father's surname was different from his. An awkward moment followed. A couple of eejits at the back of the class sniggered. Lawrence's face turned even redder than usual. Then, too late, the brother moved on.

The second vignette came on another occasion, in English class, when we were asked to write about 'the place you would most like to be'. I made up something about wanting to be a beach in the sun: a complete fraud, because I had never been on a beach in the sun back then, nor had any desire to be, and have found little interest in sunbathing ever since. But it was the sort of thing you thought you should enjoy.

Whereas Lawrence wrote about wanting to be in the woods somewhere, cutting timber with his father. The eejits at the back sniggered at that too. And yet listening to him read it, you could smell the forest and the sawdust. Which taught me a small lesson about writing. Unlike most of the rest of us, Lawrence was telling the truth, about something he knew.

In general, though, he struggled at school. I know that, because he reminded me in 2020. He still regretted having chosen the academic stream: '1A', as it was called in first year, as opposed to the more vocational '1B'.

I think it was his mother who aspired to the respectability of the former. Lawrence thought it a mistake from which he hadn't recovered. Woodwork and metalwork might have 'set me up', he told me. Instead, whenever he had an essay to write for school the next day, he'd be 'up half the night'.

Apart from the occasional sniggers at the back, he was treated kindly in school. The local St Louis convent girls were nice to him too. I recall, at a 'Halloween Hop', the annual afternoon disco where many young hearts were tenderised, watching convent girls ask him out to dance and feeling like a leper by comparison. Even if they were patronising him, he clearly enjoyed it.

My mother half-adopted him, meanwhile. I think she

bought him a jumper for Christmas one year (something that, again, I could have done with myself). We always sent him a Christmas card too.

The Leaving Cert came and went. A bunch of us then repeated, while Lawrence went back to border country and whatever life had in store for him. And I'm still slightly haunted by the last time I saw him back then.

One day after school, as usual, I was sitting with friends in the local Greenmount café (the 'Greasemount' we called it, a bit unfairly), when he passed our table on the way out. It was market day in town and he had been in for 'the dinner', obviously.

'Well, Lawrence,' we said, the standard South Monaghan greeting. 'Well, boys,' he replied. But no one asked him to join us – the booth was full – nor did he linger to chat. We were already becoming strangers again. I hoped to catch up with him in the street afterwards, but by then he was gone.

After I moved to Dublin and got wrapped in my own struggles, we lost touch completely. He was still living at home, I think. But I know now that when his mother died a few years later, he had some kind of mental breakdown.

There was poitín involved and neighbours were worried. I heard it said he was known to 'howl at the moon' on occasion. At some point, after his mother's death presumably, he had moved into a small prefab – rural social housing. His problems there included rats, he told me.

So one day, a garda dropped by for a chat and suggested that maybe he'd be better off being minded somewhere. After that, he spent 20 years in St Davnet's psychiatric hospital ('the Garage', as novelist Patrick McCabe called it, where the narrator's mother in *The Butcher Boy* went to get 'fixed').

But Lawrence had his own little house there and was free to come and go. It seems to have been a happy time, despite everything. Only after a fall two years before we met again was it decided that he needed nursing care.

His several letters to me after that first one were a scattergun collection of school reminiscences, fragments of remembered poetry, personal philosophy and warnings to be careful in Dublin. I'm not sure he had ever been to the city himself. It must have seemed a dangerous, faraway place.

He was comfortably institutionalised by the time I met him in 2021. My visit coincided with the home's early dinner time – it was late afternoon – so our long-awaited reunion had to wait another half an hour, while I sat in the common room.

When he finally arrived, he didn't recognise me. I was taller than he expected and had to reassure him it was me. From there, he gradually relaxed into memories of school, including people that I had forgotten completely but who still loomed large in his world.

As in the letters, he was scattered but thoughtful. He still read a bit, clearly. So at the end of our hour together, I gave him some books along with a box of chocolates and left promising to visit again soon.

I had planned to return in September 2021 and wrote beforehand to ask if there were any other books he would like. Alas, as with my friend Steve earlier that autumn, there would no time for a second visit. Covid got to Lawrence before I did. When I heard the news, it was too late even to attend his funeral.

In the years since school, he had become known

universally as 'Larry'. There was some comfort in reading all the tributes on RIP.ie, from people who knew him in his later life and had fond memories. One expression came up a lot and, however clichéd, rang true. He was, everyone agreed, a 'gentle soul'.

Soft Day in South Galway: On Running the National Cross-Country Championships (Over-50s)
16 February 2018

I woke up last Sunday thinking of the famous closing passage from James Joyce's 'The Dead'. This was partly because of the weather, which was broadly similar to what Gabriel Conroy experienced in the story:

> A few light taps upon the pane made him turn to the window. It had begun to snow again. He watched sleepily the flakes, silver and dark, falling obliquely against the lamplight. The time had come for him to set out on his journey westward ...

That was the other thing: I too had to set out on a journey westward. Not on a voyage of self-discovery, like Conroy, but because, during temporary leave from my senses recently, I had been talked into membership of a team competing at the All-Ireland Masters Cross-Country Championships at Clarinbridge, in the (always fiercely competitive) men-old-enough-to-know-better category.

So I dragged myself out of bed and had several mugs of strong coffee. Then I packed a rucksack for the expected arctic conditions. Then, still bleary-eyed, I checked my watch and, no longer quoting Joyce, muttered: 'F**k! I'll miss the bus.'

Snow was not general all over Ireland on this occasion.

It was falling neither on the central plain, nor the Bog of Allen, nor indeed into the dark, mutinous Shannon waves. But no sooner had we crossed that great river – which took longer than usual because of recent rains – than the ground turned white.

Soon afterwards, so did the air. It was through a blizzard that we headed into South Galway. And I braced myself again for what lay ahead: frozen ground, wind-chill factor, numb toes.

Then instead – lo! – the snow cleared. And by the time we arrived at the venue, we were once more among green fields. Even the wind had died.

The sun now glinted cheerfully on the thermal blankets of the juvenile athletes, who had already raced. Conditions seemed downright pleasant. I had not yet noticed the mud.

The first hint of that was from a veteran who returned from the course with advice about shoelaces. 'Double-knots today, lads,' he said. Somehow neither this, nor the general appearance of the field, prepared me for the horrors to follow.

I will never know the privilege of competing in the National Ploughing Championships, tractor or horse-drawn. Having survived the cross-country course in Clarinbridge last Sunday, however, I now have some insight into what that must be like, even for a horse.

Speaking of horses, cross-country races often start with an equine metaphor: the so-called 'cavalry charge'. Not this time. The expected gallop was replaced by mass squelching sounds as 250 pairs of running spikes sank simultaneously into the ground, interspersed with sucking noises as they tried to get out again.

'Jesus, it's a bit soft here,' we all thought, looking forward to the first rise in the course, where the ground would surely harden. Instead, when we reached the climb, the muck climbed too. And so it continued.

The squelching was interrupted only by the occasional splash, where the rains had not yet found a vacancy in the soil. Otherwise, mud was general, all over Clarinbridge. Even at the highest point of the course, there was no escape. It was still ankle-deep, just more glutinous.

First came the shocked realisation that there would be seven kilometres of this. Then I went through all the classic stages of bad-weather running: denial, anger, bargaining, a promise to take up golf instead soon, etc. After that, gradually, a sort of acceptance set in.

Battling onwards through the quagmire then, I thought of the unfortunates who used to have to fight wars in this stuff. No wonder, amid all the horrors of the trenches, it was the mud that drove so many to despair. But on a lighter note, occasionally, I saw competitors who were suffering even more than me. That's always cheering. Somehow, eventually, I managed to finish.

Runners did indeed lose shoes on the course, at least temporarily. And I hope the organisers counted all the participants in and back, otherwise I'd fear for some of the juveniles.

Remarkably, thanks to the double-knots, my shoes stayed on throughout, although I had to scrape so much of South Galway off them at the end, I could have grown potatoes in it.

As we set out on our journey back eastward Sunday evening, I was still traumatised by my non-Joycean mud epiphany. It was a big relief to get back on tarmac. It was even nicer, a few miles north of Clarinbridge, to see snow again.

Being John Lonergan
(and other Honorifics)

OUT FOR A RUN IN the Phoenix Park one day, I met a cyclist – Lycra-clad, as in the cliché – whose smile of recognition forced me to slow down and then stop. 'It's yourself,' he said, clearly delighted to see me. 'How many years has it been?'

I had no idea who he was, but that's not unusual in my case. So already, from defensive habit, I was smiling back in apparent recognition, while playing for time and trying to remember to which of the overlapping communities I call my life this man belonged.

Current workplace? No. Former workplace? Maybe. Old YMCA five-a-side that ran for decades until decrepitude caught up with us all? I didn't think so.

Then I realised he was talking about Mountjoy Prison, in the 1990s, and some sort of race he had run while there. He was also recalling a photograph of the occasion and wondering if he could still get a copy: 'I'm after turning my life around. It'd be nice to have.'

A penny dropped, or seemed to, here. I had been in Mountjoy once, for something. Not a race, but maybe an event related to it. I must have covered this for *The Irish Times*, hence the photo. No, he had said. The picture had not been in any newspaper: 'It was just a mugshot, in the prison.'

That's when I changed my smile of pretend recognition to one of embarrassed regret. 'You know, even though you *do* look familiar,' I lied, 'I'm afraid you're mixing me up with somebody.'

He was already nodding in agreement. 'Yeah, I was thinking the same thing. I was just saying to myself: "Mister Lonergan's looking very fit for his age."'

Turning this mixed compliment over in my mind afterwards, I wondered how long it had been since John Lonergan, former governor of Mountjoy, had retired. A decade at least, and that was after a 40-year career. Whereas I was about 53 when the man in Lycra mistook me for him.

Then again, he was picturing the governor at the time they knew each other, I suppose, now frozen in memory. Anyway, I congratulated the cyclist on turning his life around, as I'm sure Mister Lonergan would have done, wished him continued luck with it and jogged on.

The scenario has repeated itself on several occasions since then. Every so often, a stranger on the street will address me as 'John' or 'Sir'. And knowing now who they think I am, I give them a sympathetic nod in return.

Once, it was a man sitting on the footpath, with a Styrofoam cup in front of him, begging. I wondered if I should stop and chat with him, as perhaps he expected. But then I'd have to explain that I wasn't the ex-governor, really or – worse – pretend I was. A friendly smile in passing seemed the best option.

It also happened on the Luas one evening. That time, though, the other party was in on the joke. A man of 70, and somewhat drunk, he addressed me as 'governor', repeatedly. But he knew I wasn't the governor, really. 'Nice man,' he added.

John Lonergan does seem to have been universally liked by his former charges. I've never met him in person, but in TV and radio interviews he always comes across as an empathetic person, with deep insights into human nature.

Which is just as well for me. Still, you'd worry that even a nice prison governor must have made a few enemies over the years. If so, I hope I don't run into any of them in a dark alley some night.

***

I wouldn't claim to suffer from prosopagnosia – face blindness – exactly, but I may at have at least a mild form of the condition. This was first revealed many years ago on the night of my Leaving Cert party.

The girl I brought to it was not well known to me. I had mainly admired her from the opposite side of the local main street, which is a wide one.

But the invitation needed to be done up close, in the middle of a footpath, on a market day, while my friends engaged *her* friends in diversionary manoeuvres nearby, a situation so nerve-wracking it should have etched every detail on my mind.

Between that and her picture appearing in the local newspaper around the same time, I had in the intervening days become emotionally involved with the arrangement of her facial features. Or so I thought.

Then the big night arrived. Another friend, Gary, was bringing someone from the same area and had his father's car, so we went together.

And just as we were arriving at my date's house, we passed a young woman, walking, who turned and smiled, clearly expecting us. She was only a little familiar to me, I realised. And there was good reason for that – we had never met before.

But as I grinned gormlessly, Gary looked from her to me and said: 'Is this …? And I was about to blurt 'Yes', when – thank God – she rescued me. 'No, I'm her sister,' she said. The terrible thing is, when we saw the two together, they were not especially alike.

My poor grasp of faces is one of many reasons I never went into politics, despite a family background in the trade. A similarly afflicted (in both senses) friend tells an instructive story about her and her mother running into a well-known Fianna Fáil politician – we'll call him 'Donie' – in a hotel somewhere, 30 years after he had met the mother, once and briefly.

He was having his dinner at the time (the middle of the day, naturally). But in seeing them he paused, did a quick scan of his mental photo library, and remembered that the mother was 'Betty' and the daughter 'Sarah'.

Then, as the *pièce de résistance*, he asked the former: 'How is Willie getting on?' Willie was Betty's husband, and a Fine Gael councillor of many years. It was, as Sarah says, an awe-inspiring display of what sets Irish career politicians apart.

Some of us struggle with faces. Some with names. The cyclist I met in the Phoenix Park that day had a photographic memory, but no time-lapse mechanism. If you can put all these skills together, logging faces, names and family relationships of complete strangers, there's a good chance you'll end up taoiseach.

***

Walking home along – yes – a dark alley one night, I met a couple going in the opposite direction, the male half of which did a double-take, stopped and recognised me. No, not as John Lonergan this time. 'Are you Frank McNally?' he asked.

I pleaded guilty, wondering as usual if we'd met before somewhere and if I should pretend to remember this while waiting for a clue as to his identity. But no, we hadn't met. He was just a long-time reader who knew me from the photograph. First he said some nice things. Then he added: 'I also saw you in the Secret Bookstore this afternoon. Have you been in town all day?'

This was worrying. Not the being in town all day part – I do that a lot. No, just the idea that I had been unwittingly identifiable to him and others, perhaps at times when I was picking my nose, or adjusting intimate body parts, or in a state otherwise uncurated for public view.

From long experience, my working assumption is that even regular readers do not recognise journalists from byline pictures. This is in part because the pictures are often hilariously out of date anyway. The worst examples are like Dorian Gray in reverse: portraits preserving an illusion of eternal youth while the realities become daily more grotesque.

But perhaps many more people do recognise us than let on, whether because of shyness or a fear of being intrusive. Or maybe because, as a Cork friend recalled of an occasion when she and others ignored Bono some-where: 'You wouldn't want to give him the satisfaction.'

Again, though, experience tells me that two minutes on television makes you more visible to strangers than 10 years of byline pictures. Some people don't seem to notice the latter at all.

Strange to say, however out of date mine have been at times, people have often expected me to be older in person. Maybe they just say that to be nice, but if true, it might have something to do with writing style.

Many years ago now, I had to give a talk to a group

of Irish expats in Brussels. I wasn't used to public speaking then and was petrified. So as the hosts and I entered the hotel lift to ascend to the venue – it was on the 32nd floor – I might as well have been an eighteenth-century French aristocrat in a tumbril on the way to the guillotine.

My forlorn hopes included the possibility that the elevator might break down and trap us in the lift for the weekend. A more realistic prospect, also comforting, was that nobody would turn up for the talk.

Then, as the lift doors closed, a distinguished-looking woman who had followed us in said: 'I'm really looking forward to this. If he's as entertaining in real life as on the page, it should be good.'

I stared at her a moment in genuine wonder as to who she meant. Then the penny dropped (with the sound of a distant guillotine blade), fraying my nerves further. When I broke it to her how dull the guest speaker was in real life, she seemed almost hurt: 'Why do you say that?'

At which point, the host intervened to introduce us. 'I expected you to be sixtyish and wintry,' the woman confessed afterwards. I was about 43 and Indian-summery at the time. My byline pic was even younger: barely in its mid-30s, I'd say.

***

Life has many ways of making you feel suddenly older. One of them – unless you're an actual prison governor or other professional authority figure – is hearing yourself described as 'sir' for the first time.

I'll always remember where I was when it happened: out running in a Dublin park, past a football pitch where there was a youth game in progress. The ball was booted across the sideline, in my general direction. So the player nearest appealed to me to kick it back, using a one-word honorific that, outside commercial contexts where it doesn't mean anything, had somehow never been applied to me before.

At first, in the Dublin accent, it sounded like he was saying 'Sore'. And that was a fair enough description of how I felt at the time, as a middle-aged runner trying to get back into shape. To his apparent question of 'Sore? Sore?', I could easily have answered: 'Yes, I am a bit – thanks for asking.'

But by then I realised he was conferring a title: the same one, presumably, he had been taught to use with his team manager and other senior figures. In effect, he was addressing me with the respect due for the perceived vast age difference between us.

There was a time when the promotion would have been more welcome. As a boy I was occasionally offended by being called 'avick' (from the Irish *a mhic*), the standard address to youth by men of my father's generation.

It was always meant affectionately, but often it was laced with unwanted concern for your tender years. 'Give me that, avick,' you would be told if seen trying to lift something too heavy. Being in a hurry to grow up, you didn't always appreciate such protectiveness.

Then there was 'master': the strange title that appeared before your name on any letters or cards you might get at the time. It seemed as old-fashioned, even then, as the mysterious 'Esq.' that followed my father's name on official correspondence.

But I was impatient to get rid of it too, and become a 'mister', as soon as possible. Mind you, in contexts other than letter-writing, 'mister' is a dubious honorific in

Ireland. Only native-born Dubliners use it as a spoken form of address: usually again when there is an age gap.

And the respect it implies can be a thin veneer, in my experience, especially when the speaker is a street-wise city kid. 'Mister! Mister! Your fly's open' is not untypical usage to a passing stranger.

'Pal' is another thing you don't necessarily want to be called in Dublin, its implication of friendship notwithstanding. In some contexts – for example the question 'What are you going to do about it, pal?' – it can be the verbal equivalent of a bottle waved in your face.

Local context is always important. In parts of Ireland, 'scoby' seems to be an affectionate form of address, although according to my Hiberno-English dictionary it means a 'rough, uncouth youth'. Maybe I missed the intended insult any time it was levelled at me, but I always took it to be no worse than 'boss' or 'horse' or the various other things you could be called in Meath.

Getting back to 'sir', it is of course used all the time in shops and in the sort of phone conversations that may be recorded for training purposes. It doesn't count for much there, however. If anything, when overused, the word can be just a distancing mechanism, a politer version of 'talk to the hand'.

In fact, even when pronounced as 'sore', by teenage or 20-something Dublin footballers, the implied respect can be shallow. Running past that same football pitch on another occasion, I was again asked to return the ball, except that this time it went behind me and I wasn't stopping. This was before I got my eyes lasered, so I was quickly demoted from 'Sore' to 'speccy bollocks'.

Thanks to running, by the way, and around the same

time as I was first knighted by that young footballer, I also became a 'master' for the second time in life.

In a moment of weakness, I got talked into being part of a team for what is euphemistically titled the Dublin 'Masters' cross-country championships. For that, you must be at least 35, or in our category 50. I was tempted to call some of the younger participants 'avick'. As for myself, after a lung-bursting sprint to finish 239th, I was definitely 'Sore'.

A Pilgrimage to the Past

IN ALL THE YEARS SINCE those terrible events in a forest near Ballinamore, I had never got around to visiting the place where my friend Gary Sheehan died. It took Gary's belated conferring with a Scott Gold Medal for bravery in 2021 to remind me this was unfinished business.

One day soon afterwards, leaving Dublin later than ideal on a December afternoon, I finally set out on the winding road to Leitrim, for a sort of pilgrimage. The drive there turned into an unexpected refresher course in Irish republican history, at least after I left the motorway in Longford.

From the jumble of possible routes north of Edgeworthstown, Google Maps sent me first through the village of Ballinalee. This had recently been immortalised by a Bob Dylan song, 'I Contain Multitudes'. Before that, it was synonymous with a hero of the War of Independence, Seán MacEoin, 'the Blacksmith of Ballinalee'. MacEoin represented the winning side of republican history. His local statue depicts the Free State general he became, before a successful political career as a Fine Gael TD and minister.

Next on my route was Ballinamuck. This was the other side of republican history, where General Humbert's early successes in 1798 – the 'Year of the French' – came to a crushing end, with disastrous results for his poorly armed Irish followers. A tourist map commemorates their doomed heroism in various locations: 'Gunner McGee's last stand'; 'Humbert surrender and Croppy grave'; 'Many Pikemen killed here'.

From Ballinalee and Ballinamuck, I continued onwards to their near namesake, Ballinamore. But by the time I reached the outskirts, the December sun was already setting, so I bypassed the town itself and, a mile or two farther on, on the road towards Enniskillen, turned left into the hills.

Up ahead was a young woman in a hi-vis vest, running with her dog. She stopped to face the car and hug the dog close. Waving to reassure her, I slowed to a crawl in passing. The GPS informed me that Derradda – the place always referred to in news reports of the 1983 events – was two kilometres ahead, then one. Then, suddenly, it was behind me, even though I hadn't noticed any landmarks.

So I did a U-turn. But when I stopped the jogger and her dog again, winding the window down with apologies, she told me I hadn't missed anything. Derradda was just a 'post office location', she said. Then I remembered the name of another wood, which had never been mentioned in news reports of the Don Tidey kidnap but had featured prominently in the Scott Medal citation: 'Drumcroman'.

'You're looking for the place Phil Meehan was shot?', the woman asked.

'Eh, no,' I said, never having heard of Phil Meehan, 'I'm looking for where a friend of mine was shot, actually.'

She paused as if wondering whether to say something, then instead gave me precise directions: 'Up past the church and left at the crossroads'.

The church turned out to St Brigid's of Corraleehan, picturesquely located on the low side of the road. It was there that, in an infamous news report of 1983, RTÉ's Brendan O'Brien attempted to interview locals about the kidnap and its aftermath. The way they said 'No comment' became a pre-internet meme, echoed all over Ireland.

But I was still wondering who Phil Meehan was. Then, just beyond the church, there was a monument to him. As I now learned, he was the first victim of Ireland's nineteenth-century Land War, shot dead near this spot in 1880 while trying to prevent a landlord fencing off property.

The landlord pleaded self-defence and was acquitted. Before the shooting, witnesses claimed to have seen him and his bailiffs running 'very fast' towards Ballinamore, while being chased by a group led by Meehan, who was carrying a 'graip' (a three-pronged fork).

But the monument is illustrated with the picture of a pikeman: the symbol of an earlier conflict. That's because, remarkably, it also mentions Meehan's unnamed grand-father, 'killed at the Battle of Ballinamuck 1798'.

And for good measure, it includes Meehan's grand-nephew, John Joe Martin, a veteran IRA man who was interned by Éamon de Valera's government during the 1940s and, having been a militant republican to the end, died (peacefully I presume) in 1972.

Three members of one family, spanning six generations and implying an unbroken link between 1798 and, however tenuously, the modern Troubles.

You could see how that version of history appealed to the Sinn Féin members who erected the memorial in 2003. Making a note of this, while wondering if there was a memorial to Gary anywhere, I continued the short distance to the crossroads and, in the gathering gloom, turned left for Drumcroman Wood.

***

In the opening chapter of John McGahern's *The Barracks*, Garda Sergeant John Reegan returns home from a bicycle tour of duty, drenched and moody, on 'a night not fit for a dog to be out in'. Asked by his wife where he has been, he reluctantly volunteers the information: 'Round be Derrada.'

Derrada (sometimes spelt with three Ds) is McGahern country. His family were one of several in the area who originally lived in Northern Ireland, as weavers, but were driven south by sectarian violence, to scrape a living on the slopes of Sliabh an Iarainn, the 'Iron Mountain', instead. The writer's parents married in Corraleehan Church.

The Barracks is largely autobiographical. McGahern's father was also a sergeant, although the real-life garda station they occupied was in Roscommon. Like the fictional schoolboy Willie Reegan, the future novelist probably grew up listening to the cynical banter of policemen warning him to stick to the books lest he too end up in 'the Force'.

My friend Gary had not grown up in a barracks, but his father Jim was a garda detective and as a child Gary must have imagined being one too. By the time we left school, though, that was not the plan. He worked for a while with the Wrangler jeans company in Galway, then for the Western Health Board. I think his longer-term hope was the banks. But in early 1980s Ireland, employment prospects were bleak, and when the Gardaí advertised for recruits, it was the obvious fall-back.

At his posthumous award of a Scott Medal for bravery, the citation noted that, although not fully trained, Gary was part of a joint Garda–Army team, alongside the equally ill-fated Private Paddy Kelly, that entered Drumcroman Wood on 16 December 1983. There, they 'proceeded to search very difficult terrain made up of dense undergrowth [...] impenetrable except from crawling on their hands and knees'.

Thirty-eight years later, I finally retraced the fatal footsteps that brought Gary to McGahern country that day. There was no sign announcing Drumcroman wood, nor did Google Maps seem to be aware of its existence. I found it only through detailed directions from the jogger with the dog.

I was also unsure if this was Coillte-owned property or private. Even so, at the only obvious entrance, I climbed over a locked gate. Darkness was falling, but it's not a big forest, so I followed the gravelled path in.

Of the dugout's location, I had no idea. But that hardly mattered. Generations of pine trees had come and gone in the intervening years. I just stopped in the middle of the woods for a few moments, in the profound silence of a December dusk, and remembered my friend. Then I offered up an agnostic's prayer and hoped somebody somewhere was listening.

***

During my belated visit to Derradda and Drumcroman, I was disappointed by the absence of any monument, even a plaque, to my old schoolfriend. Private Paddy Kelly, killed alongside him in December 1983, was equally uncommemorated. Wilfully or otherwise, Leitrim appeared to have forgotten these two young men, one unarmed and only half-trained, who gave their lives to save Don Tidey.

But some people there had long memories, clearly. As well as the remarkable memorial at Corraleehan to three generations of the Meehan family, Sinn Féin had also erected one in Ballinamore to John Joe McGirl (1921–1988), a former chief of staff of the IRA and a TD in the 1950s. Whenever there was militant republican activity in this area during his lifetime, December 1983 included, McGirl would always have been what gardaí call 'a person of interest' to their inquiries.

His monument is not universally liked in a town of less radical politics than some of its hinterlands. But it stands there nevertheless, proudly declaring him 'an unbroken and unbreakable Fenian'.

The contrasting lack of anything to remember the two young men killed when saving Don Tidey in 1983 was an embarrassment to many in Ballinamore. It must have been an embarrassment in certain high places in Dublin too.

When I mentioned it in an *Irish Times* column in 2021, someone claiming to be from the Department of Justice contacted me anonymously to say that he would make it a personal mission to have a memorial erected in Leitrim in time for the 40th anniversary.

This might have happened anyway. The Scott Medal award added to the moral pressure for something. So did *The Kidnapping* (2023), a book jointly written by my *Irish Times* colleague Ronan McGreevy and Tommy Conlon of *The Sunday Independent*: both from Leitrim and both determined to absolve a stain on the area's reputation.

In any case, it finally happened. A monument by local artist Jackie McKenna was unveiled outside Ballinamore Garda Station on 16 December 2024, 40 years later.

It comprises two pillars, one representing the Garda Siochána, the other the Defence Forces. A circular hole straddling the centre of the pillars symbolises the void left by the deaths of the two men. The concentric ripples radiating out from this suggests the still-reverberating impact of their loss.

Seeds of Destruction:
On Becoming a Nuclear Threat in my Old Age
13 September 2023

AT THE BODY SCANNER IN a Romanian airport during the summer, I set off the alarm, but not in the usual way. There was nothing in my pockets and the security people, looking alarmed themselves, didn't even pat me down to check.

Instead, I was made to go back through the machine again, then the neighbouring one, with the same result. After that, they asked me to stand aside and wait for the man who dealt with situations such as this.

My first-ever strip search appeared to be imminent. But when the man arrived, he just asked in broken English if I had 'attended a procedure' recently. I nearly said no – that I'd attended a literary conference, on Flann O'Brien. Then the penny dropped. He meant a medical procedure.

'Yes!' I remembered cheerfully, delighted to have found the correct answer: 'I was treated for cancer – prostate cancer – a couple of months ago. Is that what set the alarm off?'

Here was something clearly not about a bicycle, to reference Flann. Even so, it had an element of *The Third Policeman*, because it was about molecular interchange.

The cancer had been caught early and in a mild form, so they were able to treat it with a thing called brachytherapy. This involves injecting small, weakly radioactive seeds into the prostate via the perineum (a part of the body intimately connected with bicycle saddles), whereupon the decaying material kills any bad cells while not harming good ones.

I'd been through several airport checks since, including one on the way to Romania, uneventfully. But either this machine was more sensitive than others or I had just hit peak radioactivity.

Either way, my interrogator wanted to see a letter from the doctors, which I didn't have. Nor could I find a relevant email in my phone.

So, bringing me into an office where he had a list on the wall, he asked if I knew which 'isotope' had been used. Whereupon, pleased with myself again, I announced confidently that it was 'Ruthenium-106'.

It wasn't. I must have seen that when first googling 'brachytherapy' and the name was impressive enough to stick. As I have since been reminded, my treatment involved 'Iodine-125', which sounds disappointingly prosaic by comparison, like a dietary supplement for cattle.

In the meantime, the airport man could not find ruthenium on his list, or anything else that rang a bell with me (as opposed to with the body scanner). So in the end, he just waved me through. I was clearly harmless, and possibly in his view gormless as well.

The episode reminded me that, as a teenager back during the Cold War, I used to deputise for my county councillor father at seminars in which community leaders were trained to deal with the nuclear winter that was bound to descend upon us sooner or later, when the Russians bombed Sellafield or it melted down spontaneously.

I could hardly have imagined then a future in which I myself would one day be the source of a small nuclear incident in Eastern Europe. But then again, as recently as last year, I would have struggled to imagine myself in a hospital bed.

The day I got the diagnosis, as usual, my most pressing

problem in life was how to fill the next day's 'Irishman's Diary'. I had a 12pm appointment – awkward for a mid-afternoon deadline – and the blank-page dread was rising.

Of course, if the doctor had told me I had only a week to live, I would have taken the day off. But his news was somewhat less dramatic than that, while also falling short of the threshold for the next question I always ask in times of crisis: 'Could I get a column out of this?'

Minimally invasive as the eventual procedure was, it did involve my first overnight hospital stay, not counting the vigils kept during my parents' last illnesses. I still had a concept of hospital frozen in the mid-1990s, when my father, a farmer who didn't have health insurance, was usually in a room with at least one other patient, if not several.

So when I checked in the evening before the thing, I had packed ear plugs to block out the inevitable snoring of the guy next to me, or the terrible soap opera on the communal TV. I also had a nightgown and slippers (both newly bought in Dunne's) for treks down the corridor to wherever the bathroom was.

Despite paying VHI for 30 years, I had somehow not expected to be in a private room, with my own TV and ensuite. When a man came round to take orders for the next day's lunch and dinner, I thought for a moment it was just his Dublin sense of humour.

Apart from some guilt, my experience was so comfortable I would have happily stayed a week. I walked home 24 hours after the procedure, pain-free. But I was still a little shaken by the diagnosis, decades overdue, that I was now a paid-up member of the middle class.

In Memory of My Mother:
A Painful Epiphany
5 July 2024

I DON'T BELIEVE IN AN interventionist God, as Nick Cave sang. But my late mother did and spent much of her life petitioning Him.

After becoming a widow in 1995, she and her prayer-book took over my father's old power seat in the corner of the kitchen, beside the press where for decades he kept a cube-shaped biscuit tin full of pension applications and other forms a Fianna Fáil county councillor was always being asked to fill in.

In a way, as I joked in her funeral eulogy, my mother took over his role of public representative. Except that she was interceding with no mere local authority. It was widely believed in our neighbourhood that she had a direct line to ultimate power.

Those with problems often subcontracted their own prayer jobs out to her, although she usually didn't need to be asked. She was a compassionate woman, easily moved by the plight of others. This also made her a soft touch for charities of all kinds.

My mother and I had a troubled relationship, alas. The teenage me disappointed her and she disappointed him back. I never doubted her love. But by the time I left home, there was a damaged distance between us we never completely bridged afterwards.

It was partly the religion. I couldn't pretend to believe what she did and she couldn't accept my scepticism. I know it pained her, but it pained me too that she invested so much faith and energy in something I feared was an illusion.

This made for a dilemma when I was asked to give the eulogy. I say 'asked', but actually I was ordered to give it by my sisters (there are five of them and you don't say no to those women). So I eulogised away, erring for the day on the side of my mother's beliefs. It was her funeral, after all.

Altitude was a running theme. I recalled that she had been born in a townland whose name translates as 'the hill of the saints'. But that, through marriage, it had been her fate to come down in the world – physically (her new home was nearer sea level) and in other ways (she got mixed up with Fianna Fáil).

Now she had gone back in the direction she came from, I concluded. And I hoped that, hereafter, we would all have a friend in high places. It was a bit corny, perhaps, but sincere in its own way.

I never got around to crying at her death, somehow. Maybe it was the excitement of the wake, which had a couple of thousand people visiting the house over 48 hours.

Or perhaps I just postponed grieving. That might explain why, even today, I still occasionally have the guilty thought that I should ring my mother and find out who's dead. Then I remember she's been dead herself for 13 years.

Anyway, there I was reading my *Irish Times* last Saturday when I saw that Q&A with Áine Kerr, 'entrepreneur, broadcaster, journalist' and newly appointed chair of Gaisce, the President's Award. And, well, the funny thing is that, along with being an entrepreneur, broadcaster, journalist and chair of Gaisce, Áine also happens to be my niece.

Years ago, when she was still a schoolteacher, she sought my advice on getting into journalism. As usual, I felt inadequate to answer, because my own path was so long and drawn-out, I couldn't honestly recommend it.

But Áine didn't need advice really. She went on to achieve great success in a succession of jobs by being (a) very smart and (b) working like a dog. I'm in awe of her these days. And because she's too busy ever to meet me for coffee, I catch up with her mainly through the papers.

So the Q&A was like reading about a public person. Until it came to the question: 'What do you expect to happen when you die?' To which Áine responded: 'Feel a sense of reconnecting with my Granny McNally who embodied the sense of kindness and goodness I can only ever aspire to.'

She went on to say that, at the funeral, 'I put a note in her coffin saying I'd try to do good things in her name.' Then she added: 'On the days I feel overwhelmed, I imagine her saying a prayer one very slow delayed beat behind the priest. That long beat always made me giggle in church ... my Gran always had the last word.'

Well, you don't expect to read about your mother in *The Irish Times*. And that detail about her praying technique – true but long forgotten – hit me hard. Suffice to say, last Saturday in a Dublin café, the thing about not crying at her funeral was embarrassingly redressed.

I don't know where my mother is now. I still can't quite believe in an afterlife where we all meet again. But Áine's piece was a reminder that people live on in the lives of those who knew them, at least. And that, whatever about the gods they prayed to for success or consolation, the beloved dead themselves still have great powers of intervention.

Doric Columnist: On Becoming a Public Institution

THERE ARE MANY WAYS TO write a newspaper column. Time and energy spent on the task vary greatly from person to person.

At one extreme of the methodology (as featured in *The Penguin Book of Columnists*, a 600-page compendium) was Heywood Broun, chronicler of US life between the world wars. Broun was not a man to waste time thinking or writing about his subjects. He could sometimes do so during a break in a card game, 'dashing off a column while sitting out a few hands'.

His working philosophy was outlined once at the expense of Westbrook 'Peg' Pegler, a colleague who had admitted spending as much as 'four or five hours' on composition.

'This seemed to me a shocking confession for any man who came up from a city [news]room,' wrote Broun. 'It is too much time for Peg to put in with himself. It is too much time for anybody to waste upon the works of Westbrook Pegler.

'The daily commentator who takes too much [sic] pains with his writing has insufficient energy to get out and find something to write about ... It may be all very well for Shakespeare ... but a newspaper man ought to go clanging down the street along with the hook and ladder. He will seldom be lucky enough to have a four-alarm fire come dropping down his chimney.'

Of similar outlook was Broun's contemporary Jay E. House (1870–1936), who by his own account always ran deliberately close to deadline before going to work with an energy bordering on violence.

First, he would light a cigar and spend 'as much as five minutes' considering possible subjects: 'After that I start writing. I have never been able to write in leisurely or detached fashion. When I do write I write my head off. There are dead and gone Remingtons that still bewail the beatings I gave them. And an afternoon's work takes as much toil from me physically as would five rounds in the prize ring. I get it over quicker, that's all.'

At the opposite end of the spectrum was the Australian Charmian Clift (1923–1969) who, starting in 1964, wrote a weekly column for the *Sydney Morning Herald* and *The (Melbourne) Age*. An obsessive keeper of press cuttings, readers' letters, and other sources of material, she would review these in the middle of every week before picking a subject.

'Once this was established,' according to her biographer, 'she would do a quick handwritten checklist. Next there was the mad consulting of encyclopedias, the search through reference books, the picking of family brains: what was the story that Lily used to tell so and so, and how green was such and such, and where did that line of poem come from ...

'Then she would make up five pages of densely typed notes, listing bits of information drawn from historical, scientific and anthropological sources, as well as from her extensive and eccentric general knowledge.'

Only after that came the writing: 'Again this would be a laborious process, requiring draft upon draft before all the facts, the opinions, the questions, the examples were stitched together into four foolscap pages of prose that would be ready for the Saturday deadline.'

Like most columnists, I operate somewhere between those extremes. It may be a mercy that having to write the Irishman's Diary four days a week does not allow for Charmian Clift levels of obsessiveness. But much as I'd like to dash columns off during breaks in card games, I'm afraid my method is a bit closer to hers than to those of House or Pegler.

On a typical column day, I wake up with no idea what my subject will be. Then I spend all morning trying to find one. This might include, if not clanging down the street with hook and ladder, at least walking the streets (of Dublin or wherever I am) for a while, in hopes of seeing or hearing something interesting, or having a novel thought inspired by fresh air.

More often than not, it then degenerates into a trawl of the detritus of notepads, screen pics, books, and the mountain of magazines and cuttings that build up on my desk or kitchen table to the point where avalanches often occur, in search of a topic there that hasn't been used already.

Not infrequently, still failing to find anything worthwhile, I will next resort to praying to the patron saint of columnists (whoever s/he is) for a fully formed theme to drop from the sky. And sometimes one will. But that happens about once a year, if you're lucky. The more typical occurrence is that I run out of time and then have to choose the least bad idea of those already rejected.

From there, I spend two to three hours writing a first draft. After that, I need to brace myself to read it, because, as Hemingway said so poetically, the first draft is always 'shit'. Then I rewrite it 10 or 15 or 20 times: getting rid of clichés, minimising adverbs, tightening, polishing, and other forms of housekeeping.

At the end of all that, however inadequate the subject, the piece should at least read well, and have a certain ease about it, as if I did in fact dash it off during a break in a card game.

As to what a column called An Irishman's Diary should be about, there has never been much in the way of guidance. No editor ever tells you to write on a certain topic. It would be a great relief often if they did. Then you could blame them for the inadequacies of the finished product. Instead, you have almost unlimited choice, and always enough rope to hang yourself. Apart from anything else, it's a nightmare for procrastinators.

The only clues are in the title. Your subject should reflect an Irish outlook on the world (not that it could do anything else in my case). And it should be a diary, of sorts, so about something that's happening today, or that happened on this date in the past. Or – and this is the ideal – it should involve a revelation: preferably a funny, poignant, or thought-provoking one that has just occurred to you, and you alone, for the first time.

My favourite column subjects are things you see or hear that make you think and, when you think, that connect with something else in an interesting way. Ideally, that second thing then leads to a third thing, and/or back to where you started, in an elegant train of thought that stretches for at least 800 words without straining.

But those sorts of ideas don't occur anything like often enough. So when there doesn't seem to be anything interesting happening in the world today, history is the great fall-back.

Luckily, there is always plenty of that in Ireland. It is literally under your feet everywhere you go, in townland or street names if nowhere else. It's also in the language we speak. The hidden depths of Hiberno-English have been for me a source of countless columns, often sparked by hearing myself or someone say something common-place, finding it suddenly strange or funny, and wondering: 'Why do we say that?'

There are days, inevitably, when you draw a blank, or dig yourself so far down a hole of research you can't get out of again without emergency lifting equipment. The temptation then is to make stuff up, as Broun did some-times when his 'clanging down the street' strategy failed.

Like me, when my children were younger, he got many a column out of the activities of his baby son. But he later confessed, shameless: 'To be sure there were days when the kid did not come through. Some of the brightest things he ever did in print were sheer invention.'

Another desperate strategy is writing 'the column about not being able to write a column'. The extreme precedent there is another American, Bob Considine (1906–1975) who once wrote a piece that read in full: 'I have nothing to say today.' But for the more standard version, we are again indebted to Clift. Her 1965 treatment of the theme is typically well turned, while also perhaps hinting at the depression that would end her career and life a few years later.

Twelve months into her weekly dispatches then, she admitted to a 'chronic recurring paralysis' of mind, against which her cuttings and letters were useless. 'One could let loose on that,' she wrote, mentioning one possible subject: 'But not today, somehow.'

And so the column continued, in a mantra of self-doubt, embellished by literary allusions and punctuated by expressions of guilt about the neglect of her family life. In the process, four foolscap pages were filled somehow.

Yet she maintained the tone of failure to the last line, berating herself for the time wasted when: 'What I should be doing, of course, is writing this article.'

I have never resorted to complete fiction, even about my children, contrary to what *Irish Times* readers might suspect. Not have I ever written the no-column column. But then, unlike others, I do have a safety net.

The Irishman's/woman's Diary appears six days a week. I write only four. There is usually a reserve pile of diaries from casual contributors, waiting to be placed. On the days when the best I can think of just isn't good enough, I wave the white flag to my sub-editor, always with a feeling of shame, and in the process make a stand-in columnist happy.

Oppressive as the deadlines are at times, the good thing about a daily column is that it allows for a conversation with readers. One piece is often followed by a second on the same or a related theme, with new information or insights supplied by others. There is always somebody out there who knows more about a subject than you do.

That means you get corrected a lot too. But the good thing about making mistakes, if there is one, is that the correction can sometimes give you a follow-up column. The accidental education is a benefit too. Being a newspaper diarist is like attending the Open University, in my case for 20 years, with still no sign of graduation.

An effect of the columnist–reader relationship is that there are a lot of people I've never met who think they know me. The weekend just gone, for example, out for a walk in Dublin, I stopped into a bar I rarely visit to use the bathroom and was greeted like an old friend by a stranger who started talking to me as if resuming from where we had left off the night before.

It was about Monaghan football, a subject I raise as

often as I can get away with. But the funny thing is, the man didn't introduce himself, except to say 'I'm from Roscommon.' Nor did he detain me long, which is just as well, because I was dying for a pee. It was only a few seconds' chat, ended as quickly as it began, as if we were sure to meet again tomorrow.

There's a public service aspect to the job too. People are always suggesting subjects you should write about or asking you to mention things they're doing. In this respect, being a columnist is a bit like being the county councillor my father was when I was growing up.

He too was always being approached in public, often in the middle of trying to do other things. I knew I'd gone full circle in that regard the day of my mother's funeral when, after I'd helped put the coffin in the hearse, a man came up to me with a print-out of some local history story he thought I should cover.

The fame a newspaper column confers upon one is minor compared with even fleeting appearances on television. Still, I have had at least one Dublin pub ballad written about me, something many a great broadcasting celebrity can't claim.

It arose from an incident some years ago in which I had entered a local bar one night after hours, watched the barman serve a fresh pint of Guinness to someone and then, in answer to his brusque 'Can I help you?', ordered a drink myself. Only to be told, with indignation: 'We're closed!'

Had I been a mere tourist, the breathtaking double standard might have outraged me. But I'm Irish, so apologised for my misunderstanding and left, accepting that I had breached etiquette by entering the pub after official closing and so had come from a different time zone than those already inside. Or something.

My subsequent column on the subject – which was careful not to identify the pub – also included contrasting the complete respect accorded to the then new (Irish) smoking ban with the continuing determination to flout the old (British) laws on closing time. I had heard stories from the west of people interrupting their illegal late-night lock-ins to smoke outside in accordance with the law.

Anyway, a year or more passed after that and I had not been in the pub since. Then one summer evening I brought my family there to join the crowds sitting outside. And when I ordered at the counter, the barman leaned across and asked, furtively: 'Are you Frank McNally?'

Say no, I thought, fearing trouble. 'Yes,' I blurted. Whereupon the barman steered me across the room to the proprietor. Who, it turned out, wanted to apologise for the insult previously inflicted upon me. The drinks, she now insisted, were on the house.

So successful had I been in disguising the identity of the premises in my column that another customer asked me to wait while he went home and fetched the copy of the paper it had appeared in, which he'd been saving all this time, so I could sign it for him.

Then someone else produced a print-out of the comic ballad that had been written to commemorate the incident. The rest of the lyrics are lost to me now but the phrase 'Man from *The Irish Times*' featured prominently. Alas, I don't think the song is on Spotify.

***

Journalism has been called the first draft of history. And when you take over a column like the Irishman's Diary, a near-century-old institution in Ireland's most literary newspaper, the weight of history is part of the inheritance. Then you do it for 15 or 20 years and realise that you've become a bit of history yourself.

This happened to me in a Dublin pub one December Friday night in 2019, when I stepped into a thronged O'Neill's of Suffolk Street in the hope of watching a European Rugby Cup match involving Ulster.

That was a triumph of optimism over experience. Normally the bar would have a dozen TVs on, showing various games. But this was a Friday before Christmas, and O'Neill's was in emergency mode, coping with the enormous demand for its primary product from people who wore lit-up jumpers, or were lit up themselves, or both.

All but one screen was turned off, and although the exception was indeed showing the game, on silent, there was no room at the inn for rugby supporters. I appeared to be the only one trying to watch and couldn't even find a place to stand that wasn't in somebody's way.

I was on the point of muttering 'Bah, humbug' and walking out. Then – lo! – a small clearing opened up, beside a wall I could lean against. It had a good angle on the TV and, crucially, access to the top of the cigarette machine, where a pint might be rested.

So I established a beachhead there. And no sooner had I done that than two other rugby refugees sidled in next to me. The clearing was suddenly a huddle, border-line uncomfortable, because we were invading each other's space.

I also sensed my neighbours were a few pints ahead of me in Christmas spirit, so was reluctant to risk conversation. But when they both struggled to recall the name of the first try scorer, I couldn't resist saying 'Henderson'. And that was it. We were friends then.

They were brothers, both thirtysomethings from Cork. Big Munster fans, but even bigger Ireland ones: hence their proprietorial interest in Ulster. Anything that added to the greater glory of the national team was good.

And greater glory is what they expected. Even by general standards then, they were bullish about the next year's World Cup and determined to be in Japan to see it. But since attending the entire tournament wasn't feasible, the plan was to gamble on getting there for the knock-out stages and beyond.

I learned that the older brother, Niall, was home from England, where he worked in a university. That got us on to Brexit, on which he had strong and despairing opinions. The English people he worked with were all decent, but the 'empire porn' that had taken hold over there was intolerable. If the lunacy didn't stop, he could see himself having to leave.

While we were discussing that, unseen by us, Jacob Stockdale scored another Ulster try. The younger brother, Hugh, pointed this out indignantly, reminding us we were supposed to be watching a game.

But soon afterwards, by some mysterious means, the conversation turned to literature – specifically Irish literature of the mid-20th century. That ended any attempts to watch rugby.

Like me, Niall had a big interest in both Patrick Kavanagh and Flann O'Brien. He was also unusually well versed in the literary coteries of their era – it was his academic speciality – and the pubs they frequented.

We seemed to have a lot in common. But even so, when he asked me what I did, and I said I worked in a newspaper, and he said which newspaper, and I said *The Irish Times*, and he said which part of *The Irish Times*, and I said 'a thing called the Irishman's Diary', I didn't expect a reaction.

This is because the years have taught me, when conversing with people under 40, not to assume any knowledge of mainstream media, never mind particular corners of it.

But not only were the brothers very familiar with the Irishman's Diary, the older one was steeped in its history and appeared to find it hard to believe that he was talking to the incumbent anchor tenant.

The Diary archives were a crucial resource in his work, he explained. So now he was looking at me the way tourists in O'Neill's then looked at the framed (but electronic) portrait of Arthur Guinness that hung over the stairs and came alive unexpectedly by winking and making faces.

When Niall repeated 'You're joking?', I experienced a mild outbreak of imposter syndrome, which is never far away even after decades in the job.

But I protested that had it not been true, it was hardly the sort of thing I'd have thought of making up, for a laugh. Then I remembered I had proof – a hard copy of that day's newspaper – in my rucksack. So I opened the paper on the top of the Letters Page, folded it back, and held up my mugshot beside the sad reality.

I felt like a living history exhibit. But then Hugh said the nicest thing anyone can say to an ageing newspaper columnist: 'You look younger than the picture.' And there was only one possible reply to that: 'It's my round.'

Acknowledgements

Thank you to Patrick O'Donoghue for suggesting this book last year and for maintaining just the right elasticity of deadlines ever since, so that they never quite snapped, no matter how hard I stretched them. Thanks also to Isabelle and the others at Gill for their hard work and elastic bandwidth.

I'm eternally grateful to *The Irish Times* for giving me a job 30 years ago, especially Niall Kiely, news editor at the time, and overall editor Conor Brady. Thanks also to Geraldine Kennedy, the first female editor in the paper's history, for appointing me anchor tenant of the Irishman's Diary in 2006. I hope she hasn't lived to regret it.

Speaking of patience, I'm indebted to a series of Irish Times Letters Editors, including Fionnuala Mulcahy and the late Liam McAuley, who acquired me as part of their daily duties. They might have appreciated early copy from the Diarist more often than once in a blue moon. The recently retired Donncha O Muirithe was especially saint-like.

Thank you to Teresa for many years of forbearance, and to my children Roisín, Patrick and Daniel for providing me with cheap column material until they were old enough to sue. Thanks also to my siblings and extended family for all their support, and especially to Bernie, the youngest and (against stiff opposition) bossiest of my five sisters, for lighting fires under me when necessary.

I'm grateful to all my friends, including Sarah for her advice and positive thinking, and Fiona for keeping me humble. Thanks also to Miriam, Kim, my running pal Des and my agent Faith for all their encouragement. Finally, a big thank you to K, the hardest-working lawyer in Europe. Among other acts of generosity, she regularly lends me her eagle-like eyes, free of charge, without which recent instalments of the Irishman's Dairy would have had even more typos than usual.